BREAKING INTO COLLEGE

BREAKING INTO COLLEGE

THE UNDERGROUND PLAYBOOK
FOR COLLEGE ADMISSIONS

JEB WHITE, Esq.

LIONCREST
PUBLISHING

BREAKING INTO COLLEGE

The Underground Playbook for College Admissions

ISBN   978-1-61961-705-6 *Paperback*

   978-1-61961-706-3 *Ebook*

Dedicated to my family, who inspires me to pick fights with the unjust Goliaths of our times.

To Mom, Dad, and my loving, full-of-life children Finnegan and Siena.

And to my beautiful wife, Jilian—you are my everything.

CONTENTS

"Success is not counted by how high you have climbed but by how many people you have brought with you."

—WIL ROSE

ACKNOWLEDGMENTS

I begin by acknowledging God's guidance and grace. I feel deeply grateful for the life He has given me. I pray that my failures and successes become lessons for others.

This book is dedicated in part to my amazing wife, Jilian White. Silly, we will always be each other's cheerleader. I love loving you.

To Finnegan and Siena—Daddy loves you so much. You should always fight for those who can't fight for themselves. Because of you, our world will be a better, happier place.

To Mom and Dad—thank you. No matter the circumstances, we never had a shortage of love and encouragement.

Thank you to my longtime friends and law partners Marcella Auerbach and Ken Nolan. Your extraordinary legal careers have recovered billions of America's stolen tax dollars, exposed egregious corporate frauds, and saved lives. Your integrity is a model for our legal profession.

Thank you to all the people who helped bring this book to life: Publisher Kathleen Pedersen encouraged me to step forward as an author. Editor Ronnie Lipton is a literary magician, for she miraculously made sense of my nonsense. Book developer Kevin Murphy brought order to my ramblings.

A special thank you to my best friends, Sid Suri and George Segeda. Gentlemen, you both believed in me when I didn't believe in myself. I pray that my children find lifelong friends like you.

The reason you are reading this book is because of the dedicated faculty and staff at The McCallie School. Nearly twenty-five years ago, this prestigious, all-boys boarding school opened its doors to a Kentucky boy with no money and even less patience. You took a chance on me when so few would. The remainder of my life is dedicated to paying your generosity forward to others.

Finally, my deepest thanks to you, the reader, who, by reading and practicing the lessons in this playbook, is paving the way for a better life.

YOUR ADDITIONAL RESOURCE

With your purchase of this book, you've earned free admission to an eight-week online video course that expands on each chapter. You can attend the course at BreakingIntoCollege.com/resources. On the website, you'll also find the latest college-admissions statistics and more resources.

INTRODUCTION

Welcome to this book. It's a good thing you're here, especially if you feel overwhelmed, even frustrated, by the pressure of getting into college. Why *wouldn't* you feel that way? Competition is fierce, costs are prohibitive, the admissions process is baffling, and your school counselor is too overworked to help you.

Some people *do* get into their first choices, but *you* may feel you must settle for whatever you can get, because too much seems to be working against you. Maybe you don't have the money, the grades, the test scores, the extracurricular activities, or the community support you think you need.

"Think" is the key word there, though, because the only thing that's interfering with your chances is *what you don't know*—about the college-admissions process and about yourself. Working with this playbook, you'll fill in those gaps, learn the secrets colleges won't tell you, and identify your unique story. You'll engage in a different, more successful approach to applying to college than you'll find anywhere else.

None of that means you can neglect your grades or avoid preparing for tests. What it *does* mean is this: Wherever you are on your college-admissions path, you'll find out what to focus on to boost your appeal to your choices. If *I* could get into a great school—even two of them—despite my background, you can, despite yours. In fact, you'll learn, as I did, the best way to get in is to use your background to your advantage.

MY INCENTIVE FOR A BETTER LIFE

The odds were stacked against my chances of going to college, let alone a great one. Until I was fifteen, my family moved nineteen times throughout the South—and never to a place where college seemed like a priority.

Those moves weren't always voluntary on anyone's part. They also weren't usually planned. One day, in my sophomore year in a rural Kentucky town, my brother and I were waiting at school for the bus when I heard, "Is that your dad, Jeb?" It was. He pulled up in a U-Haul truck. "Get in," he said. As we rode, he told us we would have until the morning to get out. Without asking any questions, we knew what that meant. It was time for Move Number Twenty.

Back at "home," my brother and I gathered the boxes we had used the nineteen times before. Packing took all night, so we made a game of it: who could pack the most boxes, and whether we could beat our own records. The next morning, as my family pulled away in the loaded truck, a police car approached the house from the opposite direction. I could see my father hold his breath and check the side mirror. The police car passed by, and Dad exhaled and said, "It's time to go."

We moved on to another town and my third school in three months. That was it for me. This twentieth move spurred my search for an escape from continual uncertainty and upheaval. Then, I had an epiphany: I realized the problems I faced day to day were what set me apart from people whose lives were without struggle. I could make that my message. That was my story.

At the time, I was too young for college, so I sent application packages to the top twenty boarding schools in the country. Each package held a highlight reel of my best football plays that year, my transcript, and a cover letter. To raise my chances of admission, I customized each letter by explaining why I was a good fit for the school. I laid my story on the line, asking whether the school might have a place for a good football player with good grades but not money.[1]

MAKING IT OUT AND *IN*

A number of schools responded, and I accepted the best offer, from McCallie, a prestigious all-boys boarding school in Tennessee. My couple years there set off a positive chain of events and the course of my life.

Earning admission to several top colleges, I accepted the University of Pennsylvania, in the Ivy League. After graduation, I worked at what is now JP Morgan Chase Bank, until I applied for and received admission to Georgetown Law.

I became an attorney specializing in helping whistleblowers recover billions of dollars from the U.S. government. I've contributed to cases that went to the Supreme Court, and I've testified for numerous legislative bodies, including Congress.

---

1   Again, this book will help you, even if your grades need improvement and you're no athlete.

That trajectory began when I was fifteen, nervous about my future, when I couldn't seem to get a foothold in my everyday world. What helped me was focusing not on the turmoil around me, but on where I wanted to go in my life.

In the past few years, looking back on those hard times, I had another epiphany: the realization that my experiences had equipped me to help other people step into their true selves as a path to better things. Then, a fundraising call from one of my alma maters inadvertently showed me the scale of the need for help.

I took the opportunity of that phone call to express frustration over the lack of diversity in the student body when I had attended the university. The fundraiser pushed back with statistics on ethnic minorities at the school, but I was talking about *socioeconomic* diversity: My classmates all came from the same elite background—the opposite of mine.

Admitting the problem, the fundraiser explained that it's rare to see students of my background reach the top of the admissions-application pile.

WHAT WORKS AGAINST WORKING-CLASS FAMILIES

At least three major obstacles keep students from lower-income families out of the running for top universities.

1. LOW ADMISSION RATES

The most significant obstacles begin with an admissions rate that's less than 10 percent at most of those schools. That low percentage is a best-case scenario rather than an equal-opportunity rate. It applies only to students whom the schools see as having certain key traits.

These traits, known as "admission hooks," include students who belong to a designated, underserved ethnic group or who are excellent athletes (needed for the college's team), developmental (children of big donors), or legacy (children of alumni). For example, the chances of legacy students getting into a top school can be two to three times greater than those of a student who doesn't have that hook. Students who can claim more than one hook improve their odds even more.

Colleges love to see all fifty states represented in their student body, which can also translate into a geographic hook for students applying from under-represented states. Colleges might have another box they're seeking to check, such as a talented visual artist, musician, or dancer. An admissions advantage often depends on a perceived degree of talent or accomplishment: a high-school state champion might get a slight admissions bump; an Olympic gold medalist, a huge one.

The admission hooks combine to chip away at the application pool for those who can't claim them, effectively reducing their chances of admission to less than one percent.

The news and the numbers get worse for people lacking not only admission hooks but financial means. For example, of the "hook-less" people fighting over that one-percent slice, the advantage goes to the ones who can pay for private admissions consultants. Their applications are more likely to work their way to the top, while the ones of students who can't afford the help tend to fall by the wayside. Admissions-committee members might not even see them.

2. CRAMMED CASELOADS FOR PUBLIC-SCHOOL COUNSELORS

Paid consultants are basically mandatory, because school counselors in public high schools rarely have the time to help. In many communities across the country, they struggle to manage student-to-counselor ratios that are as high as 400 to one. They're also dealing with students' disciplinary and family problems, which often demand immediate attention. Even if these counselors try, they just can't keep up with trends in college expectations,

That reality leads to a disparity between help and knowledge. By contrast, private schools like McCallie employ counselors who *focus on* college admissions. They can also focus on their students: compare their student-to-counselor ratio—only dozens to one versus hundreds to one. So, they have the time and the knowledge to get to know students and help them tailor their applications.

An application that is a holistic snapshot of a student, guided by hand through the process, increases that student's chances of admissions. Students without those advantages must try to compete with applications that don't make a strong case and that look like too many others.

3. PARENTS AND COMMUNITIES WITH LIMITED KNOWLEDGE AND EXPECTATIONS

What also works against students' opportunities is parents who don't understand the college-admissions process (an actual limitation) or who curb their children's aspirations (a *perceived* limitation). These limitations aren't unique to working-class parents, and they certainly don't apply to all these parents.

But the likelihood of those real or perceived limitations is greater among parents who haven't been to college and who have adopted an attitude of, "Go along to get along," "Don't rock the boat," or "Don't bite off more than you can chew." To my frustration, I often hear those phrases when I work with lower-income families.

That "No more than you can chew" attitude becomes evident in students' course choices. In discouraging students from taking college-attracting, advanced courses they could have excelled in, parents demonstrate and share a "fixed mindset."

That mindset tends to rub off on their children. Students pick up the idea that a less-than-stellar test score defines them: if they don't get a certain score, they've doomed their chances at a better school. A fixed mindset prevents students from reaching out of their comfort zones toward challenging activities, leadership opportunities, and college selection.

Too often, school systems in lower-income communities reinforce a fixed mindset. They advise students that it's not "reasonable" or "realistic" to dream beyond their current means. When students look around their community, as I did, they see people adrift and going on welfare, not to college. *That* outcome becomes what's "reasonable" and "realistic" for them. But although it's difficult to look beyond the bounds of a community, it's *possible* to do so.

From higher-income families, schools, and communities, I'm more likely to hear a "growth mindset," a belief that nothing is out of the reach of a student who makes the effort. They then reinforce that philosophy with practical help. They help their students tell a resonant story—highlighting the impact of their extracurricular activities, such as work projects and community service.

Disparities in income, knowledge, attitudes, and opportunities struck me as un-American—an injustice I needed to fight.

HOW I ESCAPED A FIXED MINDSET
DESPITE EVERYTHING

Parents have enormous power to help students minimize and overcome limitations. Despite my family's challenges, my parents instilled a growth mentality in me. They told me where I was "now" was not where I was going to be. They told me that I could be the author of my story. They helped me believe the American Dream was possible for people who worked hard. I learned those lessons at home, even when that home was a motel room, as it was from time to time.

As a fifteen-year-old leaving our nineteenth residence in that moving truck, those lessons helped me form the question that kept going through my head: "How do I find solid ground?" That question, in turn, launched my dream of a better life. With my parents' encouragement, I set a direction, drove toward it, and never gave up. My story proves that you don't have to drift through life. You can set your direction and your path, and you can reach your goal.

Although my older brother learned and practiced the same lessons about hard work as I did, things played out differently for him. I think it's because he was a senior in high school during the U-Haul incident that led to my sophomore epiphany. That move didn't happen early enough for him, so he wasn't afforded the same opportunities as I was. He struggled to make a living, working crazy hours driving a cab and doing the best he could with what he had.

It was in that cab, late on a cold January night three years ago, that he died in a collision, likely caused by a heart attack. His death left two children behind.

Our mother called me with the tragic news as I waited for a limousine to take me to the first-class cabin of a plane that was to fly me across the country to settle a multimillion-dollar case. The dichotomy of our situations wasn't lost on me. I doubt I'll ever stop thinking that, if my brother could have traveled a different path, he would not have been in that cab or working those crazy hours. He would have had a more comfortable life and would still be living it.

Both of our stories, and the facts I highlight in this book, prove the importance of striving for more than you might see around you. My brother's story also teaches the need for financial stability. A college degree is still the most certain path to that.

PITTING—AND OUTFITTING—DAVID AGAINST GOLIATH (BIBLICAL *AND* LEGAL METAPHORS)

After that fundraising call from my alma mater, I became obsessed with discovering the best ways to help students earn admission to elite and competitive schools. For the next two years, I read a book a day on the application process and on financial aid. Then, I worked with students in church and throughout my community, and I saw results.

I saw time after time that what resonates with admissions committees are stories of overcoming tremendous odds—stories of struggle, determination, persistence, and grit. Students who have such a story and can present it well are likely to outshine some of those with traditional admission hooks.

If you think you don't have such a story, you're not alone. However, I've got news for you. *Everyone* has a story, and this book will help you find yours. With this book, you now have the equivalent of your own private consultant. I can help you present your case as persuasively as my firm presented the cases of our legal clients. We told compelling stories that moved judges, juries, and the federal government to act. Instead of presenting only the facts, we wove them into a storyline of inspiration and injustice that motivated action.

As an attorney for whistleblowers, I defended the "little

guy" against the "big guy." A lot of the cases involved healthcare fraud that led to patient deaths. For example, we went after manufacturers who knew their medical devices were defective, and hospitals that put profits ahead of patient safety.

Testimony and evidence helped judges and juries identify with the whistleblowers—who went to work every day wearing wires for the FBI, or getting fired, isolated, or alienated—and with the patients affected by the companies' wrongdoings. Because of those cases and that strategy, my firm protected countless patients' lives and recovered over $2 billion for the federal government.

When I began helping students get into college, I realized the same psychological principles I'd used for years in the legal world applied to the college-application process. Admissions committees are looking for the same human qualities—significance, contribution, and connection—that influence judges' and juries' decisions.

Even the material elements of the two types of cases— legal and academic—matched up: Personal testimony became student essays, the character witnesses were the teacher recommendations, and hard evidence became test scores and GPA. When I applied the legal metaphor, I had the template—and the theme that runs through this book.

Like David, who defeated the giant in the epic Bible story, and like the courageous whistleblowers who win judgments against giant organizations, you can overcome the odds of getting into your favorite college—of any size.

THE SCALE OF THE ODDS AGAINST LOWER-INCOME STUDENTS

Although "education opens doors," as the saying goes, the door to education is less likely to open to students from low-income families. *Less than half* of low-income but high-scoring students enroll in four-year schools, and they can't graduate if they don't enroll. Only *10 percent* of the people in the bottom quarter of household income earn a bachelor's degree, compared with *80 percent* of people in the top quarter.

Neatly summing up the problem is this line from *Economist* and *New York Times* columnist Paul Krugman: "Smart, poor kids are less likely than dumb, rich kids to get a degree." What's more, disparities in income and higher-education consumption *perpetuate* each other. This vicious cycle has led to the decline in social-mobility standards to an almost all-time low—Great-Depression levels, according to some studies.

Lower-income students find it tough to budge the doors of the top colleges. At Harvard University, for example, less than 4 percent of students come from the bottom 20 percent of the socioeconomic ladder, while nearly half the students come from the top 4 percent. Another study found that the top-100 high schools in the U.S., which represent only about 0.3 percent of the total number of the nation's high schools, account for 22 percent of the students at Harvard, Yale, and Princeton, three of the eight Ivy League schools.

CLAIM YOUR GOLDEN PIPELINE

Prepare yourself to fight that trend, because the most competitive schools confer the greatest opportunities and lifetime-income rewards. Studies show students from low and middle-income families who go to a top-ten college go on to earn higher salaries over their lifetimes than those at other colleges.[2] These fortunate students benefit from what's known as a "golden pipeline," leading to selective employers and graduate programs in law, medicine, and business.

I'm here to help you present your case to break into the college where your own golden pipeline is waiting for you. To accomplish that goal, we'll take a page from the

2   Study by Dell and Krueger

playbook of the "power elite": the people whose private consultants gain them coveted admissions.[3] The structure of successful applications is vastly different from the one built from most public-school counselors' advice.

That structure and that playbook should be available to everyone, and now they are. Plus, here's the best news: *You don't have to let your lack of money stop you.* **Almost all the top schools in the country offer *no-loan* financial aid.** That means you don't have to graduate with the burden of tremendous debt. That also means that you don't have to take a job that pays more but doesn't match your passion—just so you can pay off the debt.

Access to the benefits of a top school without the debt that has saddled students for generations is no longer a fantasy. The story of "if you get in here, we'll make it affordable for you" isn't being told. Universities aren't telling it, and they discourage anyone else from doing so. That lack of knowledge has discouraged countless students like you from applying to those schools.

Why *aren't* universities telling it? The president of an

---

3 C. Wright Mills coined the term "power elite" to refer to the 0.1 percent of the population that "have an unfair advantage in job selection, college admissions, control of society in general across academia, finance, military." Since 1957, when Mills wrote the book that introduced the term, the problem has become only more pronounced, as that elite's disproportionate control of the college-admissions pipeline illustrates.

Ivy League university candidly told me that *donors don't want that story to get out.* She said the feeling is that if they let "those people" in, they will reduce the number of admission slots available to the donors' own children!

Despite all their clout, donors ultimately can't keep *those people* out, because donors do not sit on admissions committees. The committee members are likely to identify with stories of struggle. Once they identify with *your* story of struggle, and you receive an admissions offer, universities *want* you to accept it. That's because they care deeply about their *U.S. News & World Report* rank. One of the key ranking factors is "yield rate": the percentage of students who accept admission offers from that school. So, they're likely to respond generously and persuasively to your request for financial aid.

WHOM THIS BOOK IS FOR

I've written this book for four audiences:

1. STUDENTS: THE BOOK'S PRIMARY AUDIENCE

This playbook speaks directly to you, the student. I wrote it for the *lower-income* student, to level the playing field—if you'll forgive a sports metaphor added to the legal and biblical ones—of getting into college. It can also help students of every other socioeconomic group tell a compelling story.

In terms of age, no matter where in your high-school years you find this book, you'll discover ways you can improve your college-admission results. The earlier you begin, the more positive influence you can have on what you present to colleges: choosing the right courses and activities, making an impact on your community, and proving you're a leader, not a joiner. Freshman year—even the eighth grade—is not too early to think about the kind of person you want to be. At the same time, senior year is not too late.

I have had the great pleasure of working with countless students over the past twenty years. I've synthesized some of their experiences into the examples in this book in the hope they might inspire you.

I also hope you'll feel encouraged that you can live the life you want, that this is possible, and that this book can help you reach that goal. At the end of the book and of the day, you're the one—not your parents and not your counselor—who needs to take the steps that will move you forward.

This book has three secondary audiences, so please excuse me for a moment while I talk directly to them:

2. PARENTS

I'm hoping this book will show you how—and how *not*—to help your children navigate the admissions process and improve their chances. By reading this book, you're already gaining a better understanding of that process. It reinforces the following advice: please avoid getting too involved in the admissions process or you'll work *against* your children, not *for* them.

I recommend you act as a sounding board, guide with a light touch, encourage them to pursue their dreams and passions (even if they conflict with *yours)*, and never lower their expectations for their future. Understand they should live their own lives. You'll help the most by knowing when to step back and have faith everything will turn out fine.

That advice extends to letting your children work through the book's exercises on their own. (You might also find value—for yourself and your family—in doing the "Mountain Self-Discovery" exercise in Chapter 1.) It might also extend to not insisting on reading their college essays: respect their preferences on that.

If you need help with resisting the temptation to over-parent, I recommend that you read *How to Raise an Adult* by Julie Lythcott-Haims.

3. SCHOOL COUNSELORS

Excessive workloads can derail your best intentions. Especially if you have hundreds of students assigned to you, you—and your students—need all the help you can get. Use this book as a tool and a resource to supplement your knowledge of college admissions and help your students succeed. To serve that vital mission, I'll distribute books free of charge to as many public schools as I'm able to. I also recommend you do the "Mountain Self-Discovery" exercise in Chapter 1.

4. TEACHERS

You have tremendous power to influence students, regardless of their circumstances, to reach their potential. The benefits of believing in them extend beyond the students themselves to their families, their communities, school administrators, and other teachers. You'll also find help with your important work by doing the "Mountain Self-Discovery" exercise in Chapter 1.

WHAT'S IN THE PLAYBOOK AND WHERE

Back to you, the student: In this book, you'll find what you need to ace the college-admissions process. You'll also find it *where* you need it, in chronological order.

Chapter 1: Case Preparation and Opening Statement: Identifying and Leading with Your Strengths

You'll start off in the same place you should begin the college-admissions process: uncovering your hidden story, talents, interests, and passions. You'll do an exercise to discover who you are as a person and where you want to be in your life. That knowledge will guide you to become and present the person colleges want in their student bodies.

Chapter 2: Jury Selection: Choosing and Affording the Right College

Next, you'll match up skills, strengths, and passions with a comfortable place you'll thrive in and can find a way to pay for. You'll learn the right questions to ask to guide you on where to apply.

Chapter 3: Hard Evidence: Clearing Academic Thresholds for Admission

This chapter will help you identify the classes and tests you should take to best position yourself for admission to that college. You'll get a better sense of what schools are possible for you at your current level. You'll also learn how to position yourself if you haven't been academically successful up to this point.

Chapter 4: Character Evidence: Making a Difference outside the Classroom

Here you'll get help in identifying impactful extracurricular activities and service and leadership opportunities that reflect your passions and help communicate your story. Admissions committees look at these activities as evidence of the value you can bring to their campus.

Chapter 5: Witness Statements: Securing Compelling Letters of Recommendation

This chapter will help you identify the teachers and the people outside your high school who can best support your story of excellence. You'll also learn how to approach them to write recommendation letters to make your story come alive.

Chapter 6: Personal Testimony: Writing Essays That Tip the Admission Scales

Your essay is your opportunity to take a stand on your own behalf and tell the admissions committee how you're unique and why you belong at the university. The exercises and advice in this chapter will help you write that story.

Chapter 7: Cross-Examination: Strengthening Your Case through Admission Interviews

If you've planned to skip these interviews because they seem too stressful, this chapter will provide compelling reasons to resist that temptation. It also will show you how to make the most of the experience.

Chapter 8: Jury Deliberation and Final Verdict: Submitting Your Application and Accepting the Right Offer of Admission

Following the advice and doing the exercises in this book should earn you a pile of acceptance letters. This chapter will help you select the school that will best propel you into your future.

CHAPTER 1

———

CASE PREPARATION AND OPENING STATEMENT

IDENTIFYING AND LEADING WITH YOUR STRENGTHS

Where admissions committees once searched for the well-rounded *student*—the Renaissance man or woman—they're now looking for the well-rounded student *body*. They're looking for people whose stories prove they can fill the gaps in those college populations. Your job, then, is to find the compelling, unique story to prove you're Student X.

Even you have such a story, and even you can find it. When you do, that story will become your opening statement—another term borrowed from the world of law—and the theme that runs through your application package—and your life. For example, maybe you're the mathematician who built a web portal to educate people about your first love, baseball statistics.

THREE REASONS YOU MIGHT SCOFF

If you have trouble believing you have a story, it's probably because of the conflicting beliefs you hold instead:

1. TOO MUCH FOCUS ON THE NUMBERS

You—or your parents or teachers—are interfering with finding your story, because you're letting numbers define you, as this story illustrates:

Earlier this year, a frantic parent asked me to help her "*only* B+ student" with the college- application process. The mother kept referring to her daughter that way until I stopped her. Grades don't define the student, I told the parent; instead, I said, her daughter is a person with a fabulous story.

Subsequent conversations with the daughter revealed her focus on international relations and uniting people. So, her essays and teacher recommendations highlighted related leadership experiences and inspiration that ultimately earned this "only B+ student" acceptance letters from the top liberal-arts colleges in the nation.

Also, note if you have stellar grades and test scores that you *want* to have define you. By themselves, numbers won't win you a place in the Ivy League, because other numbers are working against it: There are almost 40,000 public and private high schools in the U.S., which means almost 40,000 valedictorians. The eight Ivy-League schools provide only 18,000 slots each year.

That means good grades are a bare-bones threshold you'll have to meet or exceed if your goal is acceptance to a top school. Those thresholds are easy to discover: The website of every university posts the average GPA and the SAT or ACT scores of recently accepted and admitted students.

If you're below that academic threshold, you'll probably need one or more admission hooks to be considered. If you're above it, you'll need to go beyond the numbers to make yourself stand out. You'll need a compelling story—what I call "grades-plus" factors. For example, Colin went beyond his scholastic record by proving how his admittance would benefit his chosen college. In his rural high school, which had only spotty Internet service, he approached the administration for funding to start a computer-science club. He received it, and his essay to

Johns Hopkins University described that leadership initiative ("where I am now," "where my passions lie") and his intention to do the same if he were admitted ("what I'll do for your university"). Colin followed through, founding a university club for students interested in entrepreneurial Internet ventures.

Your story of passion might be completing a community-service project, starting an after-school activity, or coming up with a great idea for a business. One student I know has a passion for helping people who have no resources or ability to take care of themselves or their homes. He expressed that passion by creating a church bulletin board called "Outreach" to match volunteers to people in need.

This is key: No matter where you go to school or what your socioeconomic level is, you can identify your dreams and frustrations, and you can figure out what to do about them. Seize those opportunities and create meaningful solutions to create a story that college -admissions committees are likely to embrace.

If you commit to this book and do the exercises, you'll have your story and boost the chances that the admissions scales will tip in your favor.

2. TOO LITTLE OWNERSHIP OF YOUR STRUGGLES

You may believe you can't make a strong case for college admission due to problems you've faced in your life. For example, maybe you earned your excellent grades while you were working a night job, or raising a child whose parents have run away or are in jail. Maybe you've turned your life around after your own run-ins with the law.

Those problems help define you and can help you win admission. So, don't be afraid to tell that story and make your problems known. As it's often said, "Make your *mess* your message." When you do, you provide the opportunity for someone to step into your inspiration and become your champion before the admissions committee.

3. TOO LITTLE ATTENTION TO MINUTIAE

Your story might be hiding in the tiny details of your life, but because they're tiny, you may be ignoring them. Instead, look closely at whether they contain elements that frustrate you. Points of frustration represent an opportunity for you to invent a solution and make that your story. In doing so, you'll demonstrate your initiative and interest in contributing to your community—qualities that admissions committees desire.

Elements of excitement, not just frustration, in your

day-to-day life can also inspire initiative. For example, I worked with a ninth grader who told me the usual story in insisting there was nothing special about him. So, I asked him to walk me through a typical day.[4] He said he often does his homework by the Chesapeake Bay. When I asked why, he said he loves watching the boats, it's quiet and relaxing there, and it's halfway between school and his house.

I gently pressed on the "why" question until he finally said, "I think I've just always wanted to sail." He mentioned it frustrated him that sailing wasn't available at school, despite its proximity to the Bay. When I asked him why it wasn't, he said he thought it was because no one had ever pushed the idea. "Well, why not you?" He gave a lot of reasons why not, but I suggested maybe he should address his interest anyway. He did, and his principal approved and funded the student's request to start a sailing club.

Even if you, like many students, go to a school where funding for even *books* is hard to come by, the sailboat story holds a lesson for you: Note which opportunities lie in front of you and how you can best step into them. Then, ask yourself, "Why *not* me?"

---

4   Parents, teachers, and counselors, please note this example of helping students highlight their passions without pushing them.

SUSPEND DISBELIEF FOR YOUR OWN SAKE

Thinking of yourself as someone with a story to tell, then finding it, will not only increase your chances of acceptance letters, it will also promote your happiness. As the application process becomes one of self-exploration, identifying your strengths, talents, and skills will set you up for life well beyond college.

Now that I hope you've begun to believe in the *existence* of your special story, it's time to identify it for your opening statement. Consider who you are, what makes you different, and what impact you have made on your community. Your opening statement should *sell* the jury—the admissions committee—on your ability to contribute meaningfully to the campus.

The following exercise—applied diligently, as early as possible, and often—will help you discover your goals and your story. It will also help you differentiate yourself from everyone else.

WHO ARE YOU? LET THE "MOUNTAIN" SELF-DISCOVERY EXERCISE SHOW YOU

These ten focusing questions, considered seriously and with full concentration, will help you direct your life toward fulfillment. I developed the questions after taking every program and reading every available book on personal development. The questions will help you find your mountain—your passion, your goal, your story, and yourself. It's the essential first step to presenting that self to colleges in the most brilliant light.

1. *What mountain do I want to climb?*
2. *Why do I want to climb that particular mountain? (What's my driving force?)*
3. *How am I going to reach the summit?*
4. *What is the summit? (How will I know when I reach it? What does success look like?)*
5. *Where am I today on my journey?*
6. *What obstacles to success have I identified?*
7. *What are the milestones on my journey?*
8. *What daily steps can I take to reach that next milestone?*
9. *Who can help me up the mountain? (Can I identify a mentor who knows the way?)*
10. *Whom can I help up the mountain?*

WHY A "MOUNTAIN"

I find mountain-climbing to be a valuable metaphor for viewing my life and the lives of the students I guide. I've become so obsessed with the sport that my bucket list includes climbing Mt. Everest: My wife and I are training to cross it off within the next ten years. Famed football coach Vince Lombardi also demonstrated a fondness for the metaphor when he said, "The man on the top of the mountain didn't fall there."

When you're choosing your mountain, pick one that's meaningful and unique to you, not like everyone else's. Although you may be tempted to write an essay about your year as a member of the baseball team, resist unless you can show something unique about your experience. Again, the numbers are working against you: there are about 385,000 high-school baseball players in the country. That too-familiar tale won't cause an admissions officer to jump up, walk down the hall, and tell a colleague: "Listen to this story. Listen to this *student*."

Colleges are looking for people who stand out in positive ways, so also ask yourself, "How does this task differentiate me from everyone else?" Find the story that only you can tell. Dig that deep on all the questions, and be precise: For example, notice that the second question is, "Why is this mountain important to *you?*"—not to your parents, not to your teacher, and not to anyone who isn't you.

Keep returning to the themes of where you want to go, why you want to go there, and how you're going to get there. The goal of the exercise is to create a results-focused, purpose-driven plan that can propel you toward a mountain that means something to you.

I recommend you handwrite your answers in a journal or a notebook. Writing with a pen on paper engages the brain differently and more personally than digital writing. However, typing on a computer or other device is better than not answering the questions at all.

Answer as honestly as you can: This exercise is only for you. Its goal is to delve deeply into yourself and your dreams as you and they are today—*without restricting yourself to what's "possible."* Stay true to yourself, and keep working on who you want to be and where you see your strengths. Make that your focus and do your best to tune out the rest of the world.

Then, every month—maybe on the same day of the month—answer the questions again. As you evolve, your statement might change over time. Each time you work on the questions, ignore what you wrote before.

THE IDEAL AGE FOR SELF-EXPLORATION

It's probably no coincidence that I was fifteen when I had the first epiphany that changed the direction of my life. The sophomore year of high school is often a critical one. Schoolwork, even in non-honors classes, becomes tougher. When faced with increased workload, challenges, and pressure, students respond in one of two ways: either they seize the opportunities, or they seize up. Students with a growth mindset rise to the opportunities, doubling their efforts.

Students with a fixed mindset do the opposite: They *expect* to fail whether they work hard or not, and failing for lack of effort seems less embarrassing than failing for lack of talent.

I want to reach students by their freshman year, so they can embrace a growth mindset as they head into that critical sophomore year.

If you're finding this book in your senior year, or just before, it might be a little late to take on a new mountain—a new task—that will resonate with a college-admissions board. (But it's not necessarily *too* late, as you'll see in at least two student examples in this book.) For you, then, the exercise becomes useful in retrospect: Reframe and answer the questions in the past tense: "What mountain *did* I climb?" "Who *helped* me?"

Start keeping track of your accomplishments today for every high school year you can recall. Note the impact you had, the people who can corroborate your story, and any other evidence you're living a life of intention.

Regardless of the age you begin, I recommend you follow my example: continue to return to the exercise throughout your life for all the other decisions that will come up, such as, "What job should I take?" "How should I spend my time?" "What are my priorities?"

NOTE: THE EXERCISE IS *HARD*

Don't worry if you find the exercise challenging. Your diligent attention to the ten questions might leave you, at least at first, without a clear sense of who you are and where you want to go. At a bare minimum, the exercise should help you identify and honor your passions. As you return to the exercise every month, a clearer picture of yourself will emerge. That's another reason to begin the process early in your high- school career.

You'll also gain insight by combining the questions in this exercise with the ones in the sidebar in this chapter. They include what your strengths are, where you see yourself in the future, and which activities so engage you that you lose track of time while doing them. What will also help are the videos and documentaries you'll find on BreakingIntoCollege.com/resources, the website that goes with this book.

CLIMBING THE WRONG MOUNTAIN

Even if you find any of the questions in the self-examination exercise difficult, don't skip them, or you might regret it as much as at least one student did. Laura didn't contact me until she was filling out college-*transfer* applications. She was unhappy at MIT, her previous first choice *despite* her dislike of both math and science. During the call, she blurted out her list of transfer choices: five or six other prestigious universities. I encouraged her to take a step back and do nothing else before the mountain exercise.

Laura pushed back, because she felt in a hurry to submit her applications. I had to explain that her previous year's hurry was probably what landed her in the wrong school. At that point, she admitted she had chased the name on the sweatshirt instead of thinking about which school would help her grow as a person.

When Laura thought in terms of where she wanted to go, she applied and was accepted at a small liberal-arts college. This low-profile school hadn't been anywhere on her initial list when she was shopping for big names.

Shopping for big names often happens when students are trying to live up to the real or perceived expectations of their parents. When I meet with parents, though, they often tell me they want only for their child to be happy. Conveying that thought in conversation to the student, though, I often hear, "Sure, they want me to be happy, as long as I get into the Ivy League." There's a disconnect there. You may be able to clear it up by talking with your parents in the presence of some outsider who can mediate and reflect what each person says.

HOW I FOUND MYSELF ON THE WRONG SUMMIT

People can choose a mountain and reach its summit, only to realize they've climbed the *wrong* mountain. They've worked hard to attain something that doesn't fulfill them. "Success without fulfillment is the ultimate failure," wrote life coach Tony Robbins. That failure doesn't afflict only students, a lesson my eight-year-old son Finnegan taught me three years ago during soccer play.

Soccer—being hands-free and requiring less precise aim than, say, baseball—permits multitasking. So, when my son asked me to play soccer with him, I agreed, as long as I could make some business calls at the same time. I thought I was the father of the year, because I was entertaining my son while participating in a phone conference.

When my conference call ended, Finnegan said, "Dad, I'm glad you're off the phone; I've got to tell you…" I cut him off, "Hang on a second; something just popped up on my schedule; I've got to take this call." I jumped on the call and kicked the ball. When it didn't come back, I looked up to see my son's eyes welling up. Then, he said the words that were like a knife through my heart: "How do *I* get on your schedule?"

The idea that I was putting the needs of a client before the needs of my son told me I needed to recalibrate my priorities. I had reached the top of the legal profession, but I didn't like the view. My schedule was interfering with my family's lives. My son showed me I had climbed the wrong mountain. That was my wake-up call, my "aha" moment.

At *this* moment, three years later, I'm at home with my children in the next room. In a half hour, we'll go to the park. My recalibration led me to pursue projects that reflect my passions, including college admissions and giving back in other ways.

THE TAKEAWAY: CRAFTING YOUR OPENING STATEMENT

Whether you're beginning your high-school career, nearing its end, or even applying for a transfer, take the time to get to know yourself. Your acceptance to the best school for you is likely to depend on that process. Identify your strengths, what makes you unique, and how you can open yourself up to the admissions committee.

Then, create your opening statement to reflect what you've identified in your self-discovery. Your statement will be like one a lawyer might use in a courtroom: "Ladies and gentlemen of the jury, in today's case, you'll hear X, Y, and Z." Yours shifts to: "Ladies and gentlemen of the admissions committee, I am Student X, and I'm going to tell you my story." That story consists of a decision, a climb, and a summit.

After you talk about your decision, mention the challenges you faced and your wake-up call. Then, talk about your climb: What are your stories of growth and perseverance? People identify with stories of the obstacles you had to push through, how you did it, and the lessons you learned.

The last part is the summit—your stories of competence and contribution. The universal story of giving back adds meaning to your tale and increases your chances of admission: Committee members will see you as someone who will contribute to the college community when you arrive.

With this chapter, you're taking the *essential* first step of the college-application process. I strongly recommend you focus on this exercise and this chapter until you've developed your opening statement. It's that statement that will grab the attention of the audience and highlight your story in a compelling way. The results of this sometimes messy, sometimes therapeutic effort will inform the rest of your application, as you continue through the chapters.

If you need one more reason not to jump ahead of yourself in the book, here it is: A self-discovery-based opening statement is the thread that ties together every piece of a successful application. The other kind comes across as a disjointed collection that won't lead to acceptance.

THE FOLLOW-UP

When you have looked inside to gather your assets, dreams, and mountain, it's time to shift your focus outside yourself. Which colleges and which factors will foster your growth over the next four years? In Chapter 2, you'll find tools to help identify them.

SIDEBAR QUESTIONS: MORE HELP WITH CRAFTING YOUR "OPENING STATEMENT"

At the start of a legal trial, an attorney delivers an "opening statement": an overview of the case and a preview of the evidence. Similarly, long before filling out a single college application, you should craft an opening statement that summarizes your unique case and your evidence for admission. Although you won't actually present it to the admissions committee, your opening statement becomes an important filter as you piece together your college application. *Everything* in your college application should reinforce the points raised in your opening statement.

To craft your opening statement, answer the following questions:

1. *What is unique, exceptional, or noteworthy about your background or life experiences?*

2. *How would you best describe your academic strengths?*

3. *What are your strengths outside the classroom (for example, extra-curricular activities, community service, work experience)?*

4. *How would others describe your strengths? What specific examples or stories would they share?*

5. *Based on your current assessment of your strengths and passions, what are your plans (for example, your intended college major, plans for after college graduation, philanthropic pursuits)?*

After answering these questions, create the first draft of your opening statement by simply filling in these blanks:

"Something unique/exceptional/noteworthy about my life is [Answer to Question #1]. My academic strengths include [Answer to Question #2]. Outside of the classroom, I have made my mark by [Answer to Question #3]. Others would describe me as [Answer to Question #4]. In the future, I plan to [Answer to Question #5]."

CHAPTER 2

———

JURY SELECTION

CHOOSING AND AFFORDING
THE RIGHT COLLEGE

Just as everyone has a story, there's a college for everybody—including you. What you learned about yourself in Chapter 1 will help you find your college. In this chapter, you'll combine that knowledge of your passions and strengths with your research into schools to guide your focus toward the best college *for you*.

Start by understanding that the "best college for you" is not necessarily the most prestigious one. The best college for you also doesn't mean what's best for your parents, your friends, or the kids of your parents' friends. Instead of hunting for prestige, hunt for what's most meaningful to you, based on the details you'll also explore in this chapter.

You also might be pleased to know that the best college for you is not necessarily the *least expensive* option. You're about to find out what to look for and how to determine what you can afford: It may be more than you think.

Like the other chapters in this book, this one applies lessons I've learned in my law practice to help you with college admissions. As a legal case often begins with examining what the client wants, a similar examination begins the college search. The ultimate question becomes, "Which college has what I want, *including* an interest in me?"

IDENTIFYING WHAT YOU WANT

That big question means that your self-discovery process is far from over. Deepening it will guide you in taking on three other big questions related to where to apply:

- *Where do I want to go?*
- *Why do I want to go there?*
- *How do I expect to go about getting in?*

The very scope of those questions, especially the second one, demands detailed exploration. The following questions will help you match who you are to what colleges offer. They'll also help you avoid becoming blinded by only one attractive aspect of a college and forgetting what you most value and need.

- *What are your academic interests?*
- *What is your career interest, if you have one yet? Is that area so specialized that it's available only at some schools? Or do some schools provide better programs, courses, and professors in that specialty?*
- *How do you learn best—in a group setting or alone?*
- *What social and cultural, and perhaps religious, activities are important to you?*
- *Do you want a college that offers involvement in the neighboring community?*
- *What kind of environment do you prefer: a campus that's more diverse—however you define that—or more homogeneous?*
- *What geographic area feels best for you?*

The question of location comes down to the Big Four:

1. **Weather**: *Do you care about the climate where you'll live for four years? What, if any, influence do you expect it to have on your activities and experience?*
2. **Distance**: *Do you want to explore a new area of the country or stay closer to home?* Also consider *why* and *how*. Relationships and travel costs tend to factor into the distance decision.

3. **Size:** *Are you likely to prefer a big campus—generally offering a less personal environment and a greater course selection—a small one, or a mid-size?*

4. **Setting:** *Beyond campus size, what community size appeals to you: a big-city experience such as you'll find around NYU or Penn, the more rural (like Dartmouth) or suburban environment that a Stanford or a Princeton provides, or something in between?*

A visualization exercise might help you with these questions: When you imagine yourself on your college campus, what do you picture? For example, do you see rolling countryside or an urban setting? Are you in a large theatre-style lecture hall or an intimate classroom?

RESOURCES FOR FINDING COLLEGES THAT HAVE WHAT YOU WANT

Take your time answering the questions above, as you did with those in Chapter 1. When you've given enough thought to what's important to you, you'll start to identify the colleges that offer it. Turn to tools, many of which are free, to start matching your priorities to schools.

1. **Big Future**[5] lets you sort U.S. universities by factors you identify as important to you. For example, these

---

5 https://bigfuture.collegeboard.org/compare-colleges

might include size, location, majors, sports, other activities, and net price. Based on the criteria you input, the site will generate a list of colleges you can click on for a profile of each.

2. **College Navigator**[6] from the U.S. Department of Education is another tool to help you narrow your search to schools that meet your criteria.

3. **Niche College Search**[7] (formerly College Prowler) provides rankings and college students' reviews.

4. **College websites**. You don't need me to tell you to go to a college's website to learn about that college's majors, courses, and activities. Beyond the obvious, the websites can reflect at least an idealized image of the experience at that college. Also, read the student newspaper for leads on what the students care about. Then go offsite to students' social-media posts.

5. **"Big books"**: Of the various college-reference books, the one that most people use is the *Fiske Guide to Colleges*, which includes a profile of most U.S. universities. Although this resource is not free, many public libraries and school counselors keep a copy on their bookshelves.

6. **Sign up for the mailing list**: If you take the PSAT, ACT, or SAT, check a box, and score well enough, colleges will send you their brochures.

---

6   https://nces.ed.gov/collegenavigator/

7   https://www.niche.com/colleges/?degree=4-year&sort=best

7. **Your school counselor**: As you've learned in this book and maybe even at school, your counselor might be too busy to counsel you effectively. But that doesn't mean you shouldn't reach out. Even if you don't receive help on the spot, use your meeting as an opportunity to be *seen* and to make a good impression. You'll need that counselor to write a recommendation for you when you apply.

8. **Current college students**: Word of mouth from students who go to a school on your list can be a valuable resource. Consider finding students in your field of study to get the rundown on the quality of the courses as well as a picture of student life.

COLLEGE-CHOICE TOOLS THAT SHOW YOU CARE

Beyond resources that teach you about schools, other resources that could serve you well are ones that demonstrate your interest in a university. If a school must choose between you and a comparable student for one spot, the advantage goes to the student who has met with its rep or toured its campus. The school logically sees visitors or guests as more likely to accept an admissions offer.

1. **College reps at your high school**: Every fall, reps from many colleges travel to visit seniors at their high schools. They come to encourage applications, because

the more a school receives, the more it can decline, which improves the school's selectivity ranking. *You can use the experience to assess colleges—often several at a time.* At the start of my college search, I met reps from Harvard and Penn when they visited with along with Duke, Georgetown, and Stanford. Five of the so-called "Seven Sisters" women's colleges—Wellesley, Barnard, Bryn Mawr, Mount Holyoke, and Smith—have a similar arrangement.

2. **College reps online**: If colleges don't come to you, you can go to them at virtual college fairs. You'll have the opportunity to talk with each participating rep in that college's chat room.

3. **Virtual college tours.** If you can't afford to travel to colleges, you can take a decent tour of hundreds of colleges on CampusTours[8] or YOUniversityTV,[9] which also provides stats.

4. *Actual* **college tours**: No virtual visit, at least not so far, can match the value of actually showing up on campus. Despite the scope of a college investment, it's surprising how few students visit the colleges they end up attending. If there is any way you can manage to visit, I strongly recommend that you do so.

---

8   https://www.campustours.com/

9   https://www.youniversitytv.com/category/college/

DON'T JUMP TO CONCLUSIONS

If you can tour colleges, start with what I call the "bench test": sit on a bench on campus and observe the activity, while you consider whether you can see yourself going there. Then go beyond the bench test to get the full picture: Sit in on classes and talk with more students and professors. Take detailed notes about each campus you visit and ask your parent or other companion to help you keep track of what you liked and didn't like.

I twice received a lesson to look beyond my infatuation to each school's more permanent factors, yet I didn't really learn it until after I accepted an offer.

The first time, I was still a junior in high school. An older friend who attended a big-city university invited me to visit him there during a beautiful spring weekend. The campus and the experience were also beautiful, so I thought my college-application search was over before it had begun.

When I mentioned my positive impression to my school counselor, he showed me an article ranking the university dead last in terms of social activity—behind even the military academies. But I wanted a college life beyond just studying—although, as it turned out, I would've been better off with *less* social activity. So, my search returned to square one.

I received the lesson for the second time during my tours of Yale (my first choice), the University of Pennsylvania, and Harvard. At Yale, everything that could go wrong *did,* starting with miserable weather and our tour guide's bad mood. Those factors turned out to be nothing, though, compared with the lead story of that day's student newspaper: "Grad student murdered on campus." The night before my tour, a professor had killed a graduate student with whom he had been having an affair. That was my introduction to Yale.

The next day, I toured Penn's campus, and the experience could not have been more different: It was a lovely, unusually warm day. Blue sky. Birds chirping. Free food. Free *beer.* (The campus was inaugurating its president.) Of course, the best part was that no one had been *killed* there the night before. So, because I didn't look beyond the pretty snapshot, I saw Penn as my destiny, and that's the offer I accepted.

Although I'm happy with my experience at Penn, I realized later that my first impression distracted me from doing my homework. I needed to explore behind the snapshot to see which school would be my best fit. I urge you to do the same.

MORE TOOLS: HOW COLLEGES TELL YOU WHAT THEY WANT

As you shop around and assemble your wish list, don't go too far with any particular college until you determine whether you can meet the college's requirements. By doing your research, you can gain insight into what each college considers an ideal candidate.

1. **Press releases**: Every year, colleges boast on their websites about that year's incoming freshman class. The spotlighted qualities represent that college's points of pride. For example, a press release might mention musicians or published authors or valedictorians. In doing so, the college signals the qualities it cares about and wants more of. Check those signals not only to choose schools, but also to position yourself to your chosen ones.

2. **Naviance**[10] shows the average SAT/ACT scores and GPAs of students from your high school who are admitted to particular colleges. This would be useful if your school provides it, but few public high schools make it available.

3. **College websites** appear a second time on your resource list because they contain more than information about the academics and experience the school provides. You'll also find admissions criteria, dead-

10 https://www.naviance.com/

lines, and other application hoops you might need to jump through—and it's better to know about them early on so you can prepare effectively.

WHAT COLLEGE CAN YOU AFFORD?

Don't be afraid to tour, and apply to, schools that seem financially out of your reach, because they're probably not. That's true even though the number-one question parents ask me is, "How am I going to afford college?" It's a good question, but cost of college should never determine everywhere you apply.

Amy's story demonstrates that truth. Her parents were pressuring her to attend a local community college, at least for her first two years of higher education, because they hadn't been able to save money for college. With my encouragement, Amy applied to Cornell and Columbia, both of which matched her goals and potential *and* offered non-loan financial aid. Cornell admitted her, then provided a financial package that made it *less* expensive to go there than to a community college.

There's a good reason that this chapter began with identifying where you want to go instead of determining what you can afford: The top schools in the country have such big endowments that they are able to eliminate loans from their financial-aid packages, and that list is growing. So, when you ask, "Can I afford any of those schools?" the answer becomes "Yes"—if you have the credentials.

NO LOAN, LESS COMPROMISE

The fact that the top schools have removed loans from their financial-aid packages is a beautiful thing for our country. It means that many intelligent, hard-working, and ambitious students will graduate without the burden of a backpack full of rocks—student-loan debt. They can pursue careers that match their passions instead of taking high-paying jobs they hate, only to be able to pay off their loans.

That's a big and important "if," and it's why I urge you to start as early as you can to develop those credentials— courses, grades, impactful activities and jobs, etc. Do all you can to make top schools view you as a coveted asset for their student body, regardless of your ability to pay.

You'll also boost your chances of financial aid in the form of a grant or scholarship by making sure your GPA and test scores are in the top 25 percent of the school's profile of students admitted the year before. Of course, those grades and scores will also boost your chances of being accepted in the first place.

Universities also help you figure your true out-of-pocket expenses with a Net Price Calculator.[11] By law, every

---

11   https://npc.collegeboard.org/student/app/hampshire

school that receives federal loan money must include this calculator on its website. You can enter your family's finances, and it will calculate your potential financial -aid offer and total cost of attendance, including tuition, room-and-board, and books. The gap between the cost of attendance and your financial aid is your projected out-of-pocket expense. Universities stress that this projection is not written in stone.

To figure out your actual out-of-pocket expenses, or expected family contribution (EFC), you must go through the joy of applying for financial aid through the federal government's Free Application for Federal Student Aid (FAFSA). The federal government, not the colleges, uses this information to determine your EFC. In other words, that figure is the same whether you go to Harvard or Honolulu Community College.

However, not all financial-aid offers are the same. Some schools package the offer with burdensome student loans, while others cover all of the students' demonstrated need with grants, which never need to be repaid. Again, the top schools in the country entice their admitted students with no-loan financial-aid offers.

To better understand your family's financial situation, many private colleges have students submit a College

Scholarship Service application, or "CSS profile," which is basically a more intrusive version of the FAFSA. If your GPA and standardized test scores place you in the school's top twenty-fifth percentile for admitted students, you might earn university grant money or scholarships to cover even your EFC.

On the other hand, *private* scholarships—from non-university sources—are less likely to help. You might have seen TV commercials about available money for college that goes unclaimed. What those ads don't mention is *why* it's not claimed: Private scholarships often are too narrowly focused for anyone to qualify for them.

Even if you could qualify for a private scholarship, it wouldn't be worth your time to chase one: It would comparably reduce your university financial-aid package, because federal guidelines require you to report any private scholarship, and colleges to take it into account.

In fact, the only people that private scholarships seem to help are, ironically, wealthy students who use them to reduce out-of-pocket expenses. The average private scholarship is only $2,500 for just one year. The amount combined with the annual effort of reapplying limits the return on investment.

Spend time instead on identifying the best fit of a college that will reward you for attending. That's one in which you're in the top quarter or can receive non-loan student aid.

What if you *don't* have the academic credentials to attract financial rewards? Make sure you apply to at least one financial safety school—one you could pay for out of pocket if you need to. For many students, that's a local community college.

APPLY TO A BALANCED PORTFOLIO: SAFETY, TARGET, AND STRETCH SCHOOLS

A "safety" school—a sure thing—is one of the three categories you should apply to, based on your credentials, overall application, and financial means. It's also the category students rarely want to consider. Instead, they tend to want to apply only to the other two school types: "target"— you've got a fifty-fifty shot of acceptance—and "stretch" or "reach"—your first choices, where your chances of acceptance drop to 20 percent or less.

Those odds prove the need for safety schools, which can, in fact, be fabulous. To avoid setting yourself up for disappointment and leave room for your fondest wish, include schools from all three categories on your list. Make sure that every school on the list is a match for you. Equally important is to make sure you include only schools—even safety schools—that you would be happy to attend if one of them turns out to be your only option.

It's worth repeating my recommendation *not* to include any school only because a parent or a friend is pressuring you to apply. Ultimately, the decision to find a school that will nourish you, and where you'll feel comfortable, should be yours. It'll be your home for the next four years. If you end up at a school that doesn't fit you, it could set you up for failure and four years of misery.

Apply to ten or twelve schools—again, balanced among the three categories—to improve your odds of receiving more than one acceptance letter. Invest sufficient time to do the work required for successful applications: about 100 hours starting from January of your junior year through December of your senior year.

In Appendix 1, you'll find a timeline of activities that begin with your freshman year and get more detailed as you go into your junior and senior years. Appendix 2 is a matrix to help you keep track of the strengths and weaknesses of the various schools on your list.

THE TAKEAWAY

Your job and your homework, then, become matching what you want—based on all the factors identified in this chapter (geography, special interest, majors, and more) and in the previous one—to what the school wants. Find the school that fits *you*. While you calculate what you can afford, remember that a price tag doesn't have to cause sticker shock: Few people actually pay that price. Position yourself throughout your high-school career to qualify for a generous financial-aid package.

THE FOLLOW-UP

At this point in your process, you've assembled your list of up to a dozen colleges. A factor in the question of who will ultimately send you acceptance letters can come down to this: whether you clear your favorite school's academic thresholds for GPA and standardized-test scores. Understanding those thresholds for each college and clearing them will be the focus of the next chapter.

SIDEBAR QUESTIONS: HOW TO
CHOOSE YOUR SCHOOLS

When they select where to file court cases, attorneys look for judges and potential jurors who are likely to be most receptive to the facts of the case. As a college applicant, take a similar approach in selecting where to apply to college. As basic as it may sound, different colleges are looking for different kinds of students. If you want to receive substantial financial aid and gain entry to a particular college, you need to persuade the college-admissions committee that you're *their* kind of student. Do so by showing that the college's priorities match your unique strengths, needs, and desires.

Before you compile a list of potential colleges, answer these questions:

1. Review your opening statement from Chapter 1. *How are you different from other applicants? Specifically, what unique strengths, experiences, or perspectives do you offer colleges?* Research and identify colleges that publicly tout the existence of these traits in their student body.

2. Students have different perceived needs when it comes to selecting a college. Re-read the sections of this chapter to identify your top considerations—for example, location, size, and weather. *Which colleges from your answer to question #1 satisfy these considerations?*

3. A college education is helpful if it aids you in achieving your post-college dreams. *Recognizing that your long-term plans may change, do any of the remaining colleges on your list offer the courses and majors that prepare you for your post-college career?*

4. As discussed in this chapter, colleges offer the most generous financial-aid packages to their most coveted applicants—that is, students with GPAs and test scores in the top 25 percent of the profile of admitted students. *Would any of the colleges on your final list consider you a "coveted student" worthy of sufficient financial aid? Do any of the colleges offer loan-free financial-aid packages?*

5. Most importantly, you should be happy to attend *any* college on your list. *Could you envision yourself attending each one?*

CHAPTER 3

———

HARD EVIDENCE

CLEARING ACADEMIC THRESHOLDS FOR ADMISSION

Start as early as you can both to build and to identify areas of success in your academic profile. It's the hard evidence you'll need to make your case to admission committees.

Although you've learned that academic credentials aren't the only deciding admissions factors, they *are* the most important ones. That's particularly true for some of the more elite schools. The sheer number of applications they receive means that unless you meet the schools' academic thresholds, your application won't survive the first round of review.

By publishing the academic credentials of admitted students who have come before, colleges provide a clear sense of their thresholds. *Find and use* that knowledge. Don't be like Brian, who wasted time and energy applying to schools whose criteria he didn't meet.

By July of last year, a month after Brian graduated from high school, he had struck out on all *fourteen* of his applications. He hadn't received a single admissions offer because he hadn't done his research. Scrambling to figure out what to do, he finally asked for help. It turned out that he had applied to fourteen versions of the *same* college. Each had the identical academic threshold, which was substantially above his level.

Although Brian had top-notch essays and compelling witness statements in the form of teacher recommendations, no one saw them, because he didn't have the hard evidence to support his case. Like too many other students, he had fallen victim to the "shotgun effect," in which he shot blindly at the *U.S. News & World Report*'s "Top Twenty" list.

Brian ultimately decided to take a gap year to pursue other interests and regroup. Meanwhile, I helped him restructure his application profile and apply only to colleges that fit his credentials. That approach made all the difference: He received acceptance letters from six of the nine schools he applied to, and he packed his bags for Vanderbilt University.

FOCUS ON IMPROVING YOUR GRADES

To avoid having your grades limit your choices, do the work on the front end. Recognize the importance of grades and, often, test scores in building your case for admission.

GRADES + CHALLENGES

Take your studies and grades seriously, because colleges certainly do. Focus on maintaining your grades throughout high school. In addition to a high GPA, colleges also want to see that you've challenged yourself. Make sure you're taking the most difficult courses available.

Colleges find out whether you're taking the most difficult available courses from the "secondary-school report" that your school counselor must fill out. The bottom line is you want your counselor to check that "most-difficult-available-course-load" box. Long before report time, talk with your counselor to find out what "most difficult" means. For example, does it mean you need to take every single Advanced Placement course? It's a balancing act and a judgment call, which is still another a reason to stay in touch with your counselor.

For example, let's say you're in every Advanced Placement class and you're struggling, picking up Cs or Ds. If you're finding the courses too difficult or your workload too great, don't suffer in silence; do something about it. Reach out to your teacher. Maybe you can hold on to the Advanced Placement classes by doubling your efforts and getting help to boost your grades. Or the teacher might suggest that you move to one or more Honors classes (if they are less challenging than Advanced Placement classes at your school). Depending on the school, the grades you get in your new classes might apply to the overall semester. Seek help so you can decide what to do.

Advanced Placement classes or not, high school is a marathon, not a sprint, so depending on where you are in high school, you might still have time to improve your grades. Even if you've collected one or two poor ones, make sure you end the year and your high-school career on an upward note and be prepared to explain what you did to turn those grades around.

Beyond showing course difficulty, also show that your grades and optional classes align as much as possible with your expressed dreams and story, or reasonably explain why they don't. For example, a low grade in science or an ignored science elective is likely to raise questions about your dream of becoming a doctor. *Mis*alignment, then, could help you also *justify* a poor grade, if you have to: That same dream could be useful in explaining away a D in English.

Take heart: It's rare that a student comes to me with a pristine academic record. If that doesn't describe you either, don't try to hide it. Assume the college is going to find out, be the one to tell the tale, and be proactive: Find a way to help the admissions-committee members understand your bad grade, bad semester, or even bad year. So it doesn't become the focus, try to put it in a bigger context. If you can—assuming you cleared the academic threshold overall—the blip on your academic record might not matter.

ANOTHER WRONG MOUNTAIN LED
TO THE WRONG DEAN'S LIST

My own academic path wasn't always smooth, and I almost didn't recover. This story proves the need to take action when you find yourself struggling. If not for wake-up calls from my roommate and then my advisor, I wouldn't have learned that lesson.

When I enrolled in the University of Pennsylvania, I thought I had reached the finish line. I had made it all the way from rural Kentucky into the Ivy League. What I didn't realize was that there is *no* finish line. The race—to work hard, graduate, move on, and do well in life—had just begun.

Toward the end of the first semester of my freshman year in college, all I had to show for my struggles was a GPA of 1.7. That less-than-stellar accomplishment earned me another—a place on the dean's academic-probation list. I had spent the whole semester in classes that didn't interest me, without doing anything about it.

My roommate—watching me read about world history, political science, and economics when I should have been studying for my biology final exam—provided my first wake-up call. He suggested that I might be on the wrong track and should change my major to align with my interests.

That was excellent advice, and it arrived not a moment too soon, because I was heading for expulsion. If not for my roommate, I probably wouldn't have identified the cause and solution to the problem until it was too late. In fact, it almost was. When I approached the Dean of Academic Advising to ask to change my major from biology to political science, she put me in my place with these words: "Jeb, this university does not need you."

That's the kick in the pants and the humbling ego check I needed. I had gone from being a big fish in the small pond of my high school to being a very small fish in the very big pond of college. *Everyone* at college was smart and driven; I could no longer coast. I needed to take my academics seriously.

I pleaded for another chance and resolved to make it work this time. With a new major and that new resolve, my GPA reflected my efforts: I went from a 1.7 to a 4.0 in the very next semester, and I graduated three years later with a 3.6.

As you learned in Chapter 1, you can use such stories of struggle and overcoming odds. The compelling story of my dramatic academic climb became the opening statement of my successful applications to the top law schools in the country. In fact, that story gained me acceptance letters that friends with higher GPAs didn't receive.

(Of course, I'm not advising you to deliberately goof off at school so you can show a grade improvement. Find your own authentic, unique, and compelling story. It doesn't work to use someone else's.)

Whatever you do, avoid the path of least resistance. Although you might be tempted to take it easy in high school, keep yourself motivated and focused on your mountain. The decisions you make now will affect the rest of your life. If you're taking shortcuts on your course load, you're ultimately shortcutting your chances. Admission committees are skilled at identifying and rejecting students who only coast through high school.

Colleges also have a way of identifying high-school students who coast through *senior year.* Don't succumb to senioritis; keep your focus and your GPA up. Even after a college accepts you, it's still watching you through final, end-of-year transcripts. Based on slipping grades as well as misbehavior on the student's part, colleges have been known to rescind their offers of admission.

Admissions-committee members have also been known to *call* school counselors. In addition to checking on final grades, they might ask how projects finished up, so also keep up the extracurricular activities you put on your college application. Your storyline—before or after admissions or even for a prospective employer—should never become that you gave up on a project because you didn't think it counted.

MORE IMPACTS OF INCOME GAPS

The students who are least able to afford to coast, along with anything else, come from lower-income families. Household-income disparity leads to grade disparity in more ways than the psychological differences you saw earlier in the book. In addition to access to paid tutors, higher-income students often have more study time, access to better curricula and facilities, and a more conducive study environment than lower-income students do.

For example, when I did the limited homework assigned at my rural public high school, I had to do it on campus during study hall because of the distractions at home. Funds at the school itself were limited, so there also weren't always enough textbooks for every student. If I wanted to take a book off-campus, I had to sign for and return it.

Low funds also resulted in the availability of only one AP class, which I took my sophomore year. That meant that if I had remained at that school until my senior year, I could have argued that I had taken the most difficult classes available. But I wasn't learning anything.

The country's high-school population includes a large percentage of students who are struggling in schools with low funds and few, if any, challenging courses. They don't have equal opportunities. If that describes your situation, look into whether you can arrange to take a course or two at a local community college, at a neighboring high school, or for free online.[12] Indeed, some community

---

12 Google MOOCs (Massive Open Online Courses) or visit https://www.mooc-list. com for course listings.

colleges even offer free courses to high-school students with the hopes that the students will enroll there after they graduate from high school.

As if quality-education access were not enough to cause a deep grade disparity, there's an even uglier side of the funding story. The specter of grade inflation may be playing a role at some private schools across the country. Where parents pay teachers' salaries and make large donations, the pressure on teachers to accommodate students and their parents can sometimes affect report cards, according to a number of studies. The focus becomes not to upset parents by failing Johnny and ruining his chances of getting into his dream college.

HOW—AND WHETHER—TO USE STANDARDIZED TEST SCORES

Standardized tests are the other part of the academic metrics that colleges take into account, although, as you'll see below, they're not equally important to all schools.

Not only can these tests round out your credentials, they're still required at many schools, including many of the top ones. So, if you plan to participate, the question becomes whether you should take both the SAT and the ACT, or, if not both, which one to take.

You don't need both. Colleges view the SAT and the ACT as equivalent tests, so you could submit your score for either one to demonstrate your college readiness. To decide between them, take both *practice* tests: the PSAT and, for ACT, the "PLAN." Like some students, you might score better on one than on the other. If, for example, your ACT scores are higher, don't plan to take the actual SAT. Instead, concentrate your limited time on studying for and taking only the ACT.

There's also value in taking your chosen test more than once. Some schools let you submit an SAT or ACT "super score," your top score for each section. Of course, the tests cost money every time you take them, but the fees aren't high, and you might be able to get them waived.

THREE MORE TESTS TO SET YOURSELF APART

Additional tests offer more ways to identify yourself as a serious student and differentiate yourself:

1. **Advanced Placement (AP)**: If you take an AP class, take the AP test for that subject. That test proves, better than a grade can, that you've mastered the material at a college level. Passing the test will also earn you AP credit at some colleges.

2. **SAT-subject**: You'll also prove mastery of the mate-

rial by taking an SAT-subject test for that AP subject, in addition to the AP test.

3. **International Baccalaureate (IB)**: These tests are given to the juniors and seniors in this additional advanced program. Most colleges view the IB as equivalent to the AP program.

SKIP *ANY* TEST?

If standardized tests simply aren't your thing, no matter how often you take them, it may not be a deal-breaker to skip them. A growing number of schools have adopted "test-optional" admissions policies for all or many applicants. Find out whether your favorite schools require them, then consider whether test scores would elevate your admissions package. You can find details about this at FairTest.org.[13]

Or, if you're allergic only to the SAT and ACT, you'll be glad to know that some schools are "test-flexible," meaning that you can submit Advanced Placement or International Baccalaureate test scores.

For a lot of students, test-optional policies are a positive development, because the tests tend to measure parental

---

13 http://fairtest.org/university/optional and http://www.fairtest.org/
    half-top-100-national-liberal-arts-colleges-do-not

ne. Students who can afford a tutor or a class—such
₁e Princeton Review or Kaplan Test Prep—traditionally
re better than students who can't.

FREE AND LOW-COST TEST RESOURCES

If you want to take a test but can't afford tutors and expensive classes, you might benefit from other preparation options, including:

Some free web classes—

- For help with the SAT: Khan Academy[14] (in partnership with the College Board) has been successful in substantially raising the scores of students I've worked with.
- For help with the ACT, and vocabulary in general: Number2.com[15] has good online reviews.

Low-cost "official" test guides—

Focus on these guides, published by ACT and SAT, which contain actual tests that were given to students. You can find plenty of other guides, but they're only simulations of the tests.

---

14 https://www.khanacademy.org/sat

15 https://www.number2.com/

- *The Official ACT Prep Guide,* about $33, contains three practice tests and recommended test-taking strategies.
- *The Official SAT Study Guide,* about $22, contains ten practice tests and other preparation materials.

Without a human coach, though, a student who's working part-time and taking care of a sibling might find it hard to fit in independent-study time. Even if you have a lighter workload and more time, you'll need more self-discipline than you would with a tutor or teacher to help you stay on track.

If you're diligent about working through the materials on your own, or with a friend or a study group, you should find yourself on equal footing with those who pay for help. It's even possible you'll have an advantage over them. The expensive courses can be like trying to drink from a fire hose when all you need is a garden hose. They offer a wealth of information that basically comes down to a few tactics, which the free and low-cost test resources also reveal. If you understand and apply them, you improve your results. The 80/20 rule applies: focus on the 20 percent of activities that provide the 80-percent return.

THE TAKEAWAY

Recognize the importance of the combination of a high

GPA, a challenging course load, and high standardized-test scores. Colleges consider an "A" to be less meaningful in a less-than-difficult course. They also look for upward trends, perseverance, a confident story that aligns with your results, and any negatives turned into positives. Wherever you are in your high-school years, start now to take the steps you need to sweeten your academic profile.

THE FOLLOW-UP

If all you needed to get into college were an opening statement, good grades, and high test scores, the book could end here, but these are not enough. To flesh out your argument for getting into an elite school, your case needs other elements, including character evidence—extracurricular activities, community-service projects, and leadership examples—to support the hard evidence.

SIDEBAR QUESTIONS: ACADEMIC-CREDENTIALS CHECKLIST

Before filing a court case, an attorney needs to determine whether or not the case is even viable. Similarly, before applying to a college, you need to determine whether you have a viable case for admission. For *selective* colleges to consider your application, you must clear certain academic hurdles. That means meeting or exceeding those schools' published minimums for grades and SAT/ACT test scores.

1. *For each college on your list, what is the academic profile for the recently admitted class?* If your scores place you in the top fifteenth percentile of a college, it's a "safety" school for you; if you're in the top twenty-fifth percentile, it's a "target" school, and if you're in the top fiftieth percentile, it's a "reach" school. Your list should have an even mix of all three types of schools.

2. *Did you score substantially higher on one of the two main standardized tests—the SAT or the ACT?* If so, consider only the test with the higher score when assessing your chance for admission.

3. Assuming you clear the academic thresholds, you can improve your chances for admissions if you can explain any grades that are unusually poor for you. *Are you able to show an upward trend in your grades? Are your grades substantially higher in your desired long-term area of study? Were you dealing with extraordinary family circumstances during a disappointing semester?*

4. Colleges want to see that you challenged yourself by taking the most academically rigorous schedule available. *Does that describe your overall course load? If not, did you take more challenging courses in your junior and senior years than you did in earlier years? Did you take the most difficult courses in your desired long-term area of study?*

5. *Did you excel on Advanced Placement exams and/or SAT Subject Tests that are relevant to your desired long-term area of study? For example, if you mention a passion for marine biology, did you score a four or five on the Advanced Placement Biology exam?*

CHAPTER 4

CHARACTER EVIDENCE

MAKING A DIFFERENCE OUTSIDE THE CLASSROOM

Although character evidence is rarely permitted in criminal trials until the sentencing stage, or in most civil trials, admissions committees welcome it. Members assume that past actions suggest possible future ones. You'll improve your chances of admission with proof of your extracurricular activities, community-service projects, volunteer and paid work, and leadership impact, because that proof seems to predict your contributions if you set foot on campus.

Quality and consistency are more important than quantity, though. The mother of a freshman called me for help because she was worried about her son. She said that Paul was headed for burnout because of all he was juggling. When I talked with him, it was clear that he was even more anxious than his mother knew. He was frantically trying to check off all the boxes: community service, leadership experience, a job, GPA.

Overwork wasn't the only problem; it was also that Paul had applied no rhyme or reason to his choices. In doing what he thought he was supposed to do, he became so stressed that his grades were suffering. He needed to align his interests with his activities. He needed the Mountain exercise.

So, I asked Paul about his strengths and interests, and whether any activity made him feel inspired rather than exhausted at the end of the day. Then I stopped talking so I could *listen*. In perhaps ten minutes, he got around to telling me that he likes working with children in one of his after-school activities. Someday, he said, he might want to be a teacher. When I followed up by asking what he likes about it, he got to the core, "Kids just have this energy about them—this zest for learning I feel I had at one time. When I'm around them, I feel as though it's renewed in me."

After Paul responded to my next question about what he enjoys learning—new technology, including social media and web programs—he expressed another dream: to one day design an app "that helps people." Using another active-listening skill, I recapped: "What I'm hearing you say is you have this interest in working with kids after school, and you have this interest in technology. Is there any way those two interests could intersect?" Saying he would think about it, he went on his way.

THE POWER OF THE RIGHT QUESTION

The next morning, Paul sent me a rapid-fire series of texts—ideas that led to his creation of "Tech Kids." It's an after-school program that teaches children how to use computers and social media safely. He built it in a meeting space in his church and with computers donated by local businesses, and almost three years later, the service still thrives.

In addition to helping children and his community, Paul helped himself. By developing his passion and his focus, he could shed activities that distracted from his schoolwork and stressed him out. He gained a strong storyline, an opening statement, and character evidence: He's an initiator who built an after-school program for children in need by inspiring other people to support his vision.

Next year, when Paul becomes a senior, he can share

that character evidence in his applications, essays, and teachers' recommendations. Beyond his stellar academic record and test scores, the story of his community service sets him apart and shows his likelihood of contributing to the campus community. His story also is *consistent*: It supports his expressed goal of being a teacher.

WHAT TO DO IF YOU CAN'T START EARLY

Although early stress, a scattered resume, and a worsening GPA almost botched Paul's chances, finding a consistent story during his freshman year gave him time to develop it. As with the opening statement, character evidence can be more difficult to gather in your senior year, when you're trying to look back. But in some ways, it's also the ideal time.

In your senior year and in the summer before, you've got "Parkinson's Law"[16] working for you: "Work expands to fill the time available for its completion." One of the implications of that principle is that as people set a deadline and get closer to it, a sense of urgency and hyper-focus kick in. In that summer between junior and senior year, in particular, high-school students tend to focus on deficiencies in their applications, and they commit to do something about them.

---

16 *Parkinson's Law* is a book by C. Northcote Parkinson, originally published in 1957, that introduced the principle.

Use those three summer months for self-exploration and contribution. Consider what you've learned over the three past years that you can share with others. What counts is not where you start, but where you finish, so make sure you finish on a high note. You still have time to make a difference to your community and your applications. Find a project now that contributes.

Let's say you find your application lacking in leadership. Look for those opportunities in your activities and volunteer. For some opportunities, time might even be on your side. For example, you might have been working for the student newspaper since your freshman year, but in many schools, only juniors and seniors have a shot at the managing-editor role.

RECOGNIZING A CONTRIBUTION IN THE BROAD OR THE NARROW

No matter what your age, if your resume is spread all over the place, look for the one thing you can latch onto for your opening statement and its supporting evidence. That one thing can be small, as long as it's unique and consistent.

For example, let's say you're a "serial joiner," as Paul was. During your high school years so far, you've been involved in a dozen activities. Go line by line through your resume, and examine each activity for evidence of a contribution you made while you participated in it. For character evidence, what you received—benefit, significance, awards—tends to resonate less with admissions committees than what you gave back.

Contribution is also your goal if your resume seems too focused. I worked with a student for whom ice skating was almost a full-time job. She skated up to five hours a day, and it was the only thing on her resume. I asked her what opportunities we might find in skating. For example, "Would you able to use any part of your rink time to teach?" She said she already teaches. Children at the rink had asked her for lessons, so she takes time at the end of every practice to teach. *There* was her community service.

As with this skater and many other students, you might need only to highlight what you're already doing. You may already be engaging in community service without realizing it. You may be performing a leadership role without recognizing it, because you don't have a title. But you don't need a title to be a leader. For example, as a member—not the editor—of the yearbook staff, Doug initiated, led, and completed a project: making the yearbook available online.

IMPACT AND ALTRUISM TRANSCEND TITLES

Or you may have a title. Almost every club has a president, vice president, treasurer, and secretary. But just *having* such a title isn't enough impress a university. If you have the title, consider it only an *opportunity* to demonstrate your leadership skills, not actual *evidence* of leadership. Show, don't tell: You need to prove that your leadership made an impact and produced tangible results.

In fact, results *beat* titles. Admissions committees appreciate leadership skills proven in community-service projects. Committees also favor initiators and developers of all descriptions. Look for needs in your high school or community that you can fill through a project, an invention, or a club.

Founding something demonstrates leadership and development skills. Roger started a photography club in high school; now he's a photographer for the student newspaper at New York University. *Designing an app* is clear evidence of initiation skills. For example, Michael came up with a note-taking app that lets you dictate over your notes.

Also, in the eyes of many admissions-committee members, something that you make available for free or low cost tends to beat something for-profit. Keep in mind your audience: admissions-committee members. Many of them have foregone large salaries to stay at the university because they love it. They're altruistic, maybe recent graduates, and they want more people like them on campus.

Consider where you can make an impact on your community by helping people. Examples include volunteering in soup kitchens and homeless shelters, or doing other service projects either individually or as a member of a team.

WORK EXPERIENCE ALSO COUNTS

On the other hand, universities' love of leadership, activities, and community service doesn't mean you need to give away your time if you can't afford to. Extracurricular activities might be out of your reach, because your family depends on the money you earn at work after school hours. Needing to earn money doesn't mean your applications are doomed. There's an academic threshold, but there's no *extracurricular-activity* threshold. Never avoid applying because you haven't checked some box on the application.

Not only should you *not* discount your work experience, you can use it to stand out from others. You can develop your storyline of survival and perseverance despite financial need in your opening statement, your character evidence, and throughout your applications. Overcoming odds can be a compelling story.

More good news: Even at work, you can probably find opportunities to fulfill the role of leader, initiator, founder, or community-service provider.

A SPORTING CHANCE?

Football was my avenue into boarding school; it probably helped me get into college. Sports are likely to improve the chances for exceptional athletes, but if you're an average member of a football, baseball, or basketball team, you'll look like many other applicants unless you're recruited. If your goal is an elite college, you won't get there with your team credentials, not even if you're the team captain.

Let's revisit those numbers you saw in Chapter 1. The existence of almost 40,000 U.S. high schools means almost 40,000 football-team captains. Multiply that number by the captains of other sports teams and compare that number to not many more than 18,000 Ivy-League seats each year. Your time might be better spent on different activities in which you can stand out.

"OH *GOD* NO": IF IT'S NOT FUN, DON'T DO IT

To build character evidence that resonates with admissions committees *and* enjoy a more positive high-school experience, follow the "life is too short" rule: Of the many things to do, choose the ones—in- and outside of high school—that line up with your passions. Start building the life you want to live. Never take on a task or job that isn't fun. Remember that your time is valuable, even if you're not being paid much or at all now.

Finding the fun is the lesson of this example: A father complained that his daughter Patricia wouldn't be able to apply to any Ivy-League school if she didn't work in a research lab over the summer. He had read somewhere that those top schools "require" research-lab experience.

Patricia had her heart set on an Ivy-League school: the University of Pennsylvania. But when I asked her whether she wanted to work in a research lab, she came back with "oh God no." So, she was thrilled to hear that a lot of people, including me, had attended an Ivy-League school without ever setting foot in a lab.

What Patricia really wanted to do that summer was to fill an opening at a local art studio. I helped her persuade her father that: a) he was working with false information, and b) even correct information wouldn't have justified making his daughter miserable. She spent her last summer of high school at home happily working at the art studio. *And* she later gained admission to the school of her dreams, which has a great art department.

Choose activities based on who you are and how you want to represent yourself, not based on what you believe you should do. Questions like these can help:

- *Where do you see yourself after college?*
- *Where do you see yourself in five years? Ten years? Twenty?*
- *Who is living the life you envision?*

REACH OUT TO MENTORS

For Patricia, the person who is living the life she envisions is an art professor at Penn. It's a lot easier to create the life you want to live if you can get hints from someone further along the path, so I encouraged Patricia to contact that professor with questions like these:

- *What is the path you took to reach where you are today?*
- *What were the high-school and college activities that helped you along that path?*
- *If you could do it over, how would you do things differently?*

To further develop your character evidence, learn what

you can from mentors who are already in your life. If you don't have role models in view—or even if you do—look for them outside your life. You can find people with lives you admire in the media and on the web. We live in a connected world in which people are more accessible than ever. If you reach out to your heroes and idols, you'll gain confidence along with any advice you receive from the generous people who respond.

The natural law of reciprocity suggests that many people you contact might be willing to talk or write to you. It's a way of paying forward the people who helped them up the ladder—something you might remind anyone who needs a nudge. But of course, not everyone will respond. Contact ten people, and you might hear back from only one or as many as five. When you've politely exhausted one possibility, work on another. Don't give up. Keep working the phone, email, Facebook, and your network— no matter what its size.

Your teachers and counselors might also be able to connect you with mentors outside the academic world. For example, Mark, one of the students I advise, is interested in doing triathlons. I do Ironman events, so I suggested that he talk with the Iron Cowboy, an icon in the triathlon world. Mark spent hours searching for the triathlete's contact information. Through the man's social-media connections, the student reached him and was rewarded with an insight-packed half-hour phone conversation.

Other students have reached—and received advice from—LinkedIn founder Reid Hoffman, senators, governors, investors, CEOs, and entrepreneur/author Tim Ferriss.

Of course, your best mentors don't have to be famous to be valuable to you. For example, my wife, a gynecologist, has permitted high-school students who have an interest in her profession to shadow her, even in the operating room. And I have taken students to observe congressional hearings.

You can also find your mentors in books: I continue to draw inspiration from reading biographies of people I admire, such as Benjamin Franklin—the founder of my alma mater—U.S. presidents, and business leaders present and past, such as Steve Jobs, Steve Case, John D. Rockefeller, and Andrew Carnegie. I especially love and recommend reading autobiographies: The way people write about the path they took and what was most important about their lives is often different from a biographer's perspective.

FIND THE COLLEGE NICHE YOUR ACTIVITIES FILL

When you present your character evidence to colleges,

frame it in a way that is likely to resonate based on what you've learned about them. (If you can't, you probably need to rethink your list of colleges.)

You might achieve resonance because the college needs people to support activities or specialties it already offers. Let's say you started a jazz-dance club at your high school. You're in an ideal position to make the case that you dream of dancing with the college's world-renowned troupe.

Or, to a college with no such troupe but obvious interest in the arts in general, you might show that you're the very person to found a troupe at the college as you did in high school. In either case, you're showing interest in the school, proving you've done your homework, and offered evidence that the college is a good fit for you. Demonstrating your ability to fill a particular need at that college will increase your admission chances.

Demonstrated ability to fill a need worked for Colin, the founder of the high-school computer club you met in Chapter 1. He saw no similar clubs on the websites of his preferred colleges, so he used the evidence of the one he founded as a selling point for what he could bring to college. He shared his joy of bringing people out from behind their computer screens to talk face to face about their interests in a community setting.

By the way, Colin was already a high-school senior when he founded the club that became his ticket to college. His example shows that even senior year isn't necessarily too late to make a positive impact on the story you present in your applications.

Of course, you can't always anticipate where your interests will take you in college and beyond until you get there. Hesham Samy Alim, my roommate at Penn, whose insight helped me get out of academic trouble, loves hip-hop music and its history, while I'm a country-music fan. That difference would be enough to derail most relationships, but we not only made it work, we made it into a radio show. At 10 p.m. every Friday night, we would joke around and take turns playing whatever we wanted. Hesham also started a hip-hop club on campus.

Hip hop, a lifetime passion, led Hesham to his major in linguistics both at Penn and his PhD at Stanford University. As a UCLA professor, he now studies and teaches hip-hop culture and its impact on American society. He has also written several books and is a well-regarded speaker on the topic. It all started with a little radio show during our freshman year at college.

THE TAKEAWAY

For every Colin and Patricia, there are probably ten students who do the Mountain exercise without taking action on it. But because *you're* working with a book subtitled *The Underground Playbook,* I'm hoping you're not one of them. I hope you're willing to risk doing things differently from what a lot of other people recommend. It takes courage to tune out the noise from parents and counselors who endorse an outdated approach.

It also takes courage to spend your time on activities that energize and do not deplete you, and to position your application as I recommend. Unlike many others, I'm *not* telling you to be as active as possible. Instead, I'm saying less is more: Spotlight the one area that you're passionate about and where you can make a difference.

The onus and the opportunity are on you. Realize that you don't have to live the life that other people expect of you. By identifying your dreams, you'll often receive the support and resources you need to make them a reality. And by making your consistent, compelling, and unique story come vividly to life through your actions, you'll increase your chances of admission. You'll help the admissions committee envision you walking onto their campus.

THE FOLLOW-UP

Now that you've selected and engaged in activities that reflect your passions, you'll need witnesses to step forward and testify in writing to all the results you've produced during your high-school career. This is where your teachers' and counselors' recommendations come in, and we'll explore them in the next chapter.

SIDEBAR QUESTIONS: PROVING THE VALUE OF YOUR EXTRACURRICULAR SUCCESS

In court, an attorney often tries to sway the jury by admitting character evidence that shows the client's past good deeds. By spotlighting your extracurricular successes to the admissions committee, you make a similar argument. In your case, you will suggest that your high-school successes prove you will contribute amazing things to your college of choice. Focus on successes that are unique and that support your opening statement.

The following questions will help you present the most noteworthy activities in your high-school career.

1. *How did your decisions and actions in high school lead to notable improvements for your peers? Which of those activities support your opening statement? Where did you have the greatest impact in high school? How did you show initiative and commitment?* For example, it is not enough to be president of a particular club: demonstrate how your presidency *improved* the club. (Colleges want students who will make a positive contribution to the school.)

2. *Do any of your activities detract from the argument that you made in your opening statement? Do they demonstrate you made an impact or that you only showed up?* (Admissions committees understand that your interests might have changed during high school, but they don't embrace serial joiners.)

3. *Where did you assist your local community? What impact did you make? Did your high school require you to do community service? If so, did you go well beyond the bare minimum?* (Colleges want students who prove they significantly help others outside the school campus.)

4. What initiative have you started? What was the impact? What initiatives can you launch now, if you're at the beginning of your senior year, or in the coming months? (Admissions committees are particularly impressed by students who start a club, project, or business.)

5. *If you want to continue your extracurricular activities in college, do your targeted colleges support them? If not, do all the targeted colleges have the resources and facilities to support your launch of your activities?*

CHAPTER 5

WITNESS STATEMENTS

SECURING COMPELLING LETTERS OF RECOMMENDATION

In your college applications, as in the courtroom, you need testimony from people who can give you credibility in front of the admissions committee. Identify and approach the main witness who can corroborate your allegations and key events. This is the witness who can add dimension to your storyline and help admissions committees see the person beyond your academic numbers.

For me, that witness was the person who almost gave up on me—with good reason. As I mentioned in a previous chapter, I had neglected my coursework in college to the point where I was put on academic probation. Then it got worse: My grades dropped below the minimum, and

I was academically *expelled* from Penn after my freshman year. I approached Dean Burnham to try to explain why the school should give me a *third* chance to remain on campus.

The situation required more than an explanation, actually. It required me to build and plead my case the same way you're learning in this book. In legal parlance, I threw myself on the mercy of the court. I had to show the dean what I would look like and contribute if I could fulfill the promise of my college application.

The dean didn't even want to meet with me, but after I basically chained myself to a chair in her waiting room, she agreed to listen. I made a heartfelt argument, but the outcome could have gone either way. She ended up giving me another chance, although only under the strictest-possible conditions. I met and exceeded those conditions by changing my major and my attitude.

When it came time to apply to law school almost five years later—I had been working at JP Morgan for two years after graduating from Penn—my application story became my transformation and my fulfilled promise to Dean Burnham. No one could've been a more credible witness to corroborate that story than the dean. I didn't assume she would agree to help me again, though. As this chapter advises you to do, I approached her with a package of materials, including the law schools' recommendation-letter requirements, my activities sheet, and a resume detailing my accomplishments.

Once again, the dean came to my aid; she wrote a powerful letter of recommendation. Without that witness statement, I'm not sure I would have received admissions from some of the top law schools in the country.

WRITTEN AND EMOTIONAL SUPPORT

Dean Burnham not only witnessed my academic turnaround at the University of Pennsylvania, she actually triggered it. So, she was the ideal person to write a letter of recommendation when I applied to law school. When I requested that letter, I reminded the dean about the wake-up call she had given me years earlier, when she said, "This school doesn't need you." The dean's generosity knew no bounds; at the end of this second meeting, she said, "Every law school needs a student like you."

FIVE KEY QUESTIONS FOR IDENTIFYING YOUR BEST WITNESSES

To find *your* Dean Burnham, someone who will write a compelling letter to support your character evidence, consider these questions about them:

1. *How do they express themselves?* Think about how they communicate in class, in person, and in writing. You

need to feel confident that this person can write a literate and persuasive letter.

2. *Who witnessed an event or triumph you highlight in your opening statement and throughout your application?*

3. *Which witness can best support your presentation of the event or triumph?* Identify someone who can add details and facts to prove your argument that you've contributed to your high-school community. This is not someone who stops at "___ is a good student."

4. *Who has the most recent memory of your actions?* Approach teachers from your junior or senior years, not only because they work with a lot of students, but because your performance is still fresh in their minds at that point. It's also because they're able to testify who you are today, rather than in the past. One caveat, though: If you transformed early in your high-school years, your best witness would be a teacher who knew you before and after and who can testify to your growth.

5. *Does your application show any deficiencies that a particular witness can explain? For example, if your transcript reflects a drop in grades, is there someone who can help to put it in context, such as a family or personal-health situation?*

THE TYPES OF RECOMMENDATION LETTERS AND WHY THEY MATTER

Like essays, letters from people who know you and your work can make a difference to your chances of admission. That's particularly true for a more selective school or any committee that's on the fence about you. Recommendations fall into the three categories of the people writing them: counselor, teacher, and non-academic.

As you will for every other part of your application package, check each college's requirements regarding letters, and don't send more letters than they request—unless you're wait-listed, which we'll look at in the final chapter. Colleges typically require or recommend one letter from a counselor or other school official and one or two letters from teachers. For non-academic letters—such as from a coach, an employer, or a religious leader—the question becomes not how many but *whether* the college permits them.

Wherever in your high-school career you are at present, start today to consider counselors and others as potential supporters. If you form relationships and discuss your aspirations early, they'll be able to write more persuasive recommendations for you. Make yourself known as a person who contributes to the high-school community. That's never more essential than at a big high school with hundreds of students competing for their attention at application time.

1. THE COUNSELOR'S REPORT

The counselor's recommendation is a form called the secondary-school report, also mentioned in Chapter 3. In addition to the question of whether you took the most challenging courses, the form includes questions about the student body and the school.

What else is in the form depends on the type of school—another reflection of the way income-disparity plays out: For private schools, particularly those with low counselor-to-student ratios, these reports can be as long as five pages and go into great detail. Conversely, reports from public schools with the highest counselor-to-student ratios are one-pagers, with only "yes" or "no" questions about the student.

Help the counselor to help you, no matter what type of school you attend. Of course, the need becomes more critical if you go to a big public school and don't have a relationship with your school counselor. The way to help the counselor support your chances is to provide an activities sheet that details your high-school career. You can find an example of this sheet in Appendix 3.

Put your opening statement at the top, directly under your name, so your counselor can clearly see how you view yourself. Next, include your extracurricular activities, your GPA and any context needed to explain any of it, standardized test scores, and any other appropriate background information. At the bottom, show how you envision your future. In fact, I recommend that you start this list early in high school and keep it updated, so you don't forget anything important.

On the secondary-school report, the school counselor also must respond to questions about a student's disciplinary problems, probations, expulsions, or suspensions. If any of those are in your background, have a conversation so the counselor understands your perspective on what happened and what changes you've made since. You'll need your counselor's help in turning that negative into a positive. As you've seen in this book, a story of perseverance will often get you more traction than if you just floated through.

As to grades, it's rare to see a college application that doesn't have some blemish. In some cases, the best strategy is to avoid drawing undue attention to it. One grade blip—for example, a B- on a GPA of 3.9—isn't worth your time to explain away. An admissions committee is likely to see it *as* a blip, and it shouldn't hurt you.

But if there's a difference of at least two grades—say, a C when you usually get an A—talk with your counselor about whether you need to explain. If the drop leaves the reviewer with the question, "What happened here?" that pause will probably send your application to the denial pile.

Your school counselor will probably advise you to proactively anticipate and answer the question to put it in context. Then move on, so you can avoid making that one grade the focus of the application.

2. TEACHERS' LETTERS OF RECOMMENDATION

As you would expect, recommendations from teachers can be valuable, because they provide credible personal commentary on your academic performance—not just a focus on the grade you earned. Teachers can reflect what your application says about you. If there's a discrepancy between the story you *think* you're telling and the story you're *actually* telling, teachers' recommendations can fill in the gap. They also help you highlight a stellar academic performance without having to sound as though you're bragging or exaggerating.

The most powerful recommendation letters demonstrate how the student contributed to the classroom setting.

They specify recent examples, events, and details about the student's character, work, work ethic, and contributions—perhaps in participating in classroom discussions, helping out other students, or excelling in the projects the letter describes. For many colleges, it's the student's character that is most important, and only a recommendation can effectively show that.

Although admissions committees tend to view teachers' recommendations as *less* important than grades and test scores, they view them as *more* important than other parts of the application, such as essays, activities, and work experience. Where high academic credentials are a given—such as in the Ivy League and schools such as Stanford and MIT—strong recommendations can tip your application into acceptance.

Whom to Ask

In general, admissions committees are known to view most favorably recommendations from teachers of core courses—English, history, math, science—particularly Advanced Placement or honors. Make sure at least one of your recommendation letters is in that category.

In most cases, choose teachers *from your junior year* because they have the most recent, full-year experience with you. Find the teacher who knows you best—not necessarily the one who gave you the highest grade. It should be the teacher who can most credibly help tell your consistent story, including why you're a good fit for the colleges you chose.

For example, Julia wanted to prove her passion for science in her application to MIT. She hadn't taken a lot of science courses, though, so she needed her science teacher to promote her skills and contributions in class. (The teacher did, and the strategy worked. Julia is at MIT.)

What to Provide

When a teacher agrees to write a letter for you, provide context with the same activities sheet you gave your counselor. In addition, write a note that shows how you want to portray yourself to the school. Guide the teacher towards your main focus, as well as any positive areas you would like them to validate and any negatives you'd like them to help explain away. Suggest that they supply examples to demonstrate your achievements in class.

In the package with your activities sheet and note, include everything the teacher will need to submit your recommendations, including the recommendation forms. Sign the waiver on the form that means you won't be seeing the teacher's recommendation. Sit down with the teacher and walk through the questions and make sure the teacher knows you well enough to answer them and feels comfortable with your requests. If, at this point, the teacher hesitates in any way or mentions how many recommendation requests are piling up, take the hint to disengage and find a stronger advocate.

If all goes well, though, follow up the meeting with an email of thanks by the next day, along with something like, "And for your convenience, I've also attached the package I gave you, which outlines my request." Do all you can to make it easy for teachers to help you.

When to Ask

Making it easy for teachers to help you also means beating the rush. Recommendation requests *do* pile up, so approach your chosen teachers before the end of your junior year. Approach in person, not by text or email: You want this person to remember you. Mention how much you got out of the class and that you'll be applying to college in the fall. Ask whether the teachers feel that they know you well enough to write your recommendation. If they say yes, you've already planted the seed.

Then approach teachers again as soon as the fall semester

begins, and you have received your documents.[17] Teachers are more likely to be receptive at the start of the semester than they will be when the floodgates open. They're likely to appreciate you for not waiting until the last minute. Politely confirm their willingness by saying something like, "When we talked this spring, you seemed open to writing a letter of recommendation for me. Are you still able to do that?"

If you've moved a lot during your high-school years, time might seem to be working against you. My advice to the student who arrived at a new school at the start of senior year is the same I give to freshman: Get to know your new teachers as quickly as you can, and participate in class. When you approach the teacher for a recommendation, bring along papers and projects from the first month or two of the class as a reminder of your work.

(How to) Say "Thank You"

After teachers have submitted your recommendation, it's appropriate to thank them for their time with a small gift certificate of less than $20 and a handwritten card. Then go further to show your appreciation for their efforts: Let

---

17   August 1st is the opening date for the common college application and many schools' supplemental materials, which include recommendation forms.

them know which schools accepted you and where you intend to go. Stay in touch.

3. NON-ACADEMIC (OR PEER) RECOMMENDATIONS

This type of letter can do the most to reflect who you are. Someone who knows you and your storyline very well is often your most credible and persuasive advocate. (That's no doubt the thinking behind why some colleges, including Dartmouth, require a recommendation from a fellow student.) Engage one or two of these advocates to write a letter for you to any of your chosen schools that permit this type of recommendation.

For George, it was a letter from his *employer* that made all the difference. Even though his chosen colleges didn't encourage outside recommendations, this situation was an exception:

At the beginning of the last semester of his junior year, the student's family began to experience financial difficulties. To help out, George took an after-school job working for twenty hours a week at a UPS loading dock, and his GPA fell from a 3.8 to a 2.6. No admissions committee would have been able to overlook that drop. His boss provided the context: His letter highlighted George's work ethic and contrasted him to fellow students at a prestigious school, who had the time to study and relax.

It's worth emphasizing that "one or two letters" means *not flooding* the admissions offices. Letter-writing campaigns—often on behalf of students who fall below a school's academic thresholds—have no impact. Along the same lines, name-dropping isn't as effective as you or your parents might hope. Limit writers of non-academic letters to those who know you well. For example, a generic-sounding letter from a U.S. senator your mother knows is more likely to look desperate than impressive.

Like teachers, non-academic letter-writers will also appreciate a hand-written note of thanks and any follow-up news.

BUILDING A "CASE SUMMARY"

In the world of law, the package that includes an opening statement and the recitation of key facts and evidence, the equivalent of an activities sheet, is known as a case summary. In marketing, it's similar to what's called a brand statement. Every other industry might just refer to it as a resume. It's the summary of who you are, where you've been, and where you see yourself going. It's the jumping-off point for everything in your application, including essay topics and interview talking points.

No matter what *you* call your "case summary," share it with your recommenders, so they can be consistent with your message. Also, take the time and effort in anything you present to your "judges" to avoid careless errors like the following:

When I worked for JP Morgan, I was a manager with hiring responsibility. One college senior I interviewed did a great job in the interview. At the end, she handed me reference letters. The very first one on the stack read, "To whom it may concern, [insert name here] is an exceptional student." That blunder showed up twice more in the letter. She had not only handed me a templated reference letter, she hadn't noticed it!

Of course, you can't prevent those kinds of impressions in letters you can't see—the ones that recommenders send directly to colleges. But *this* candidate *had* the ability to read the letter, and if she had done so, she would have known that the person who provided it should not have been writing her letter.

THE TAKEAWAY

Colleges typically look to recommendations before essays to see beyond the numbers and understand who you are. So, choose recommenders who will compellingly describe why you're a wonderful student and how you contribute to the community in a specific way. At the more selective schools in particular, all applicants' academic records look similar, and recommendations can help you stand out from other applicants.

Think through whom to ask for recommendations—someone who knows you well and wants to help you—when to ask them—early—and what to provide—ease and details—to ensure your most persuasive witness statements.

THE FOLLOW-UP

Character corroboration in the form of recommendations can be vital to the college-application process. But at the end of the day, you (probably) know yourself best. Personal essays help to validate how you see the world and yourself, communicate your story in your own words, and share your unique voice. In the next chapter, you'll find out how to write *your* compelling story.

SIDEBAR CHECKLIST: HOW TO FIND YOUR BEST WITNESSES

In a court of law, an attorney calls witnesses to the stand who will best corroborate his or her client's case. The ideal witness is credible and compelling. The same is true for teacher and school-counselor recommenders. In effect, they are taking the stand on your behalf and encouraging the admissions committee to rule in your favor.

The following will help you identify people who can best support your case for admissions:

1. Brainstorm a list of your high-school teachers—from your junior or senior year—who are likely to write a positive recommendation. Colleges want to understand who you are today, not three or four years ago. But do list any teachers who taught you over multiple years; they can testify to your academic and personal growth.

2. Colleges typically value the recommendations of core-subject teachers, so include at least one recommendation from this potential witness pool.

3. Coach your recommenders to include specific examples or stories that reveal who you are as a student and person. Consider which teacher can best attest to a story that supports your case for admission.

4. Finally, consider which teacher is conscientious enough to follow through with a quality letter of recommendation. Teachers get bombarded for requests to write teacher recommendations. Also, ask early enough to beat the rush.

CHAPTER 6

———

PERSONAL TESTIMONY

WRITING ESSAYS THAT TIP THE ADMISSION SCALES

No part of the applications package tends to cause students more stress than the personal essay. It doesn't have to be that way, though, and by the end of this chapter, you'll know what to do. Sure, it's a different type of writing than you may be used to. Few high schools teach it, although they should.[18]

Look at the essay as the valuable opportunity it presents: to describe something that had an impact on your life, show your individuality, and explain why you're right for the school. The more selective the school, the more

---

18   I hope school administrators pick up the idea of a personal-essay-writing class for juniors.

weight it's likely to give the essay, especially if you lack admission hooks.

Unlike recommendation letters, the essay is where *you* take the stand on your own behalf. It's the only part of the application that you completely control. If you have a story that differentiates you from other applicants, this is where you get to tell it. By this point in the book, you should know you *do* have a differentiating story: You probably uncovered it with the "Mountain" and other exercises that led to your opening statement, character evidence, and guidance for your recommenders.

Or maybe you, like Jess, another student I advised, decided to *begin* your application process with the essay. But Jess didn't start by finding her story because she didn't believe she *had* one. "I'm nothing special," she said when she approached me for help. "I've been burdened with a boring childhood."

ASK "WHY?"

Jess and I spent the next hour talking about where she has been and what she has done. At every point, I'd ask "why," as in "Why did you decide to go there?" and "Why did you decide to do that?" The "why" exercise is useful for identifying values and intentions. Consider that question on your own or with an advisor or friend while you're going through your discovery process. It will often turn up pivotal moments in your life that led where you are today.

The "why" exercise also revealed Jess' *special* pivotal moment: While playing basketball on her school team, Jess broke her leg and needed a wheelchair. So, for the three months it took her bones to mend, she rode the school bus that had a wheelchair ramp. From the first day, her fellow riders made her feel welcome and supported. They cheered her on as the ramp lowered for her and she navigated the difficult maze of railings.

Jess became friends with students who had been going to her school all along but she had never met them. The experience made her realize that she had been viewing the world through a small lens. It also made her appreciate other people's struggles. And it opened her eyes to the variety of people who go to her school and the fact that they all share a desire to make the best of their lives that they can. She discovered her passion for helping students with disabilities the way that a bus full of students had helped her.

The story—*that Jess didn't know she had*—emerged as a result of asking "why": "*Why* did you enjoy that bus so much?" "*Why* were you disappointed, at some level, when you could no longer ride it?" Being in a wheelchair for three months is a struggle Jess overcame. That's a story. Opening her eyes to a whole world she had never thought about. *That's* a story. This newly discovered passion became the theme of her essay and entire application.

The passion also translated into a career path. Now at college, Jess is learning how to teach and integrate students with disabilities. She has also started a social group to introduce those students to other students they might not have had the opportunity to meet.

If you, like Jess, are starting the application process by writing your essay, look to her story as evidence that you too have a compelling story. You don't have to have traveled the world, gone to summer camp, or worked in a research lab to have one. In fact, the more you think *stereotypically* about "appropriate" topics for essays, the further you get from an acceptance letter. You'll have to explore the path less taken to write your unique story.

FIND COMMON GROUND

Along with exploring your own—*uncommon*—path by studying *yourself,* writing a persuasive essay also requires that you study the *school.* Learn how your story aligns with its worldview and values so you can make that case in your essay. (If you can't find common ground, don't change your story; change your list of schools.)

Showing how your story aligns with a college's values also means this: write a different essay for each school you apply to. One size doesn't fit all, and that goes for templates. Sure, you'll save time by just changing the name of the school on the same essay, but you'll also lose points and acceptance letters. The essays lack authenticity even if the student *remembers* to change the name of the college they call their dream school. (A lot of them *don't.*)

WHAT AND HOW MUCH STORY TO TELL, AND HOW TO TELL IT

To write college essays, like other forms of writing, think about content—what you'll say—length—how much to say—and style—how you'll say it. Colleges provide at least some guidelines on the first two issues, more than on the third.

CONTENT: WHAT STORY TO TELL

Resist the temptation to sit down and start writing before you've thought through the essay. Begin instead with this pre-writing exercise: First think of the greatest moment of your life—maybe the moment when you were crossing a finish line, literally or not, and raising your arms in triumph. Now, *stop* thinking about it because it would make a *horrible* essay. But that might be the essay you would write if I weren't here to stop you, because it's the essay many students write.

Flip that story. What you should write about instead is the front end of that race, or the front end of any decision that got you to that point of triumph. Zero in on when you were at your lowest and crawled up from there. I'll refer again to David versus Goliath, a story so good that we're still talking about it. To make people root for you, use your main essay to tell the story of overcoming tremendous odds and climbing that mountain. Admissions committees love these stories.

If that defining "moment" dragged on for longer than a day, pick a different story. Find one that you can thin-slice to a decision point, a line in the sand, or whatever metaphor you prefer for reaching the point of no return. Highlight the place where you decided to be a different person as a result of the experience. These are the stories that earn admissions, as long as they're unique.

For example, standing up to bullies is unquestionably brave and admirable, but it has become a too-common theme. So, an admissions-committee member might dismiss it on sight as "the bully story" unless your bully story shows unusual details or an unexpected twist. If it does, put those details or twist up front. If you save them for a big finish, no one's likely to see them. Other topics that are common enough to require unique handling include the "Four Ds": death, divorce, drugs, and depression.

In addition to finding the twist, don't sound like a victim or end on a sad note—just in case the committee members read that far. Tell an inspiring story with a positive takeaway of how you bounced back and become a better person.

Brainstorm with your friends or siblings to find some of these stories. List them and put them aside for a few days. Then look for the story that seems most consistent with your application's opening statement and put *that* one aside for a few days. Make sure it meets two main criteria:

1. Consistency with your application's theme.
2. Comfort level and *actual* appropriateness. The story doesn't need to be one your parents want you to tell. But also, don't choose something that's too personal to tell strangers. Not only might you feel uncomfortable sharing it, but the committee might also view a story that's too personal as inappropriate.

Also make sure you follow each college's essay content requirements: colleges provide question prompts. Make sure you answer the question raised along with the one that's always implied: "Tell me about yourself." So, while you're taking a stand on your own behalf, also take *a* stand. Colleges want to see that you're a person of principle. Jess didn't demonstrate that in her first draft. Instead, in responding to an essay question of what immigration meant to her, she played it safe with an impersonal discussion of the pros and cons of various policy points.

Treat that and all other questions as a window into your passions and values. One typical question is, "If you could have dinner with anyone—who's living, dead, or fictional—who would it be and why?"

PAPA SMURF GOES TO COLLEGE

No topic is out of bounds—within reason—if you can make it come alive and prove its meaning to you, as my example shows.

"If you could have dinner with anyone who's living, dead, or fictional, who would it be and why?" has been one of the University of Pennsylvania's essay questions at least since I applied to the school. My answer, "Papa Smurf"—the leader of a colony of blue cartoon characters—appalled my school counselor. He protested that I was applying to a *serious* institution. But I wrote and sent in a serious essay, explaining why the character is a great leader, the type I hoped to become.

My essay was also a memorable one. After acceptance and enrollment, I was touring the campus with other incoming freshmen—all wearing name tags. A man who was walking in our direction stopped me to ask, "Are you Papa Smurf from Kentucky?" He had read my essay as a member of the admissions committee, which told me that I had succeeded in making my essay stand out.

Another typical question—"Why do you want to attend our university?"—shows whether you've done your homework about the school, so that you can tell what it is about you that is relevant to the school. It's also a clue that you might be interested enough to accept them if they accept you.

LENGTH: HOW MUCH STORY TO TELL

Follow college requirements on essay word limits, which can vary not only from school to school, but also from year to year. In most schools, the word limits are getting smaller. In the past few years, the average required length has decreased from about 800 to 600 to 400 words for the main essay, and to about 300 words for the other essays.

Schools typically ask three to five open-ended questions. There will usually be one main essay and shorter ones in the 300-word range. Just because question-guided essays are shorter than the main essay, don't think they necessarily count less. They matter for two reasons:

1. The college writes the question, and they're looking for what the question draws out of you.
2. You're more likely to stand out from other respondents who spend less time on the shorter essays than on the main one.

STYLE: *HOW* TO TELL YOUR STORY

Write your essays in a personal, heartfelt style. I've noticed that students from working-class families tend to be less comfortable sharing a personal story with an outsider than those from more well-to-do families. Poorer families often hammer home the importance of not revealing their stories of struggle to the outside world.

But it's exactly those inspiring stories that could open the doors to elite colleges. So, tell those stories, and don't feel you have to show your parents. You're telling who you are and the influences that made you that way. It's *your* story you're writing, and achieving your best future is the reason you're writing it.

More about writing style: write in the first person, and be informal and conversational; use plain language instead of SAT words. An informal style is the one you use when you talk with a teacher. But don't sound too casual. Unlike how you might talk or write to a friend, use proper grammar, and omit emojis and text language.

Other writing tips apply. Show, don't tell—in four ways:

1. Focus on strong verbs and other powerful words.
2. Have a focus. This essay isn't meant to brag or to detail your every accomplishment at high school. Concen-

trate on a slice that is meaningful to you, summarizes your high-school career, and is consistent with the theme of your application.

3. Avoid using too many adjectives and adverbs. As an exercise, delete all the adjectives and adverbs in your first draft and see how the essay reads without them. Add only the ones the essay needs.

4. Give examples and details to demonstrate points.

Hook the reader from the opening line and end on a note that makes the reader want to know more about you. That advice is particularly valuable, because each admissions-committee member might review hundreds of applications. They probably only skim most essays, so you'd better clear the initial attention hurdles while they're sorting through their application pile.

(You hope admissions committees at least *skim* essays. When I asked one admissions officer whether he reads every essay he receives, he said, "Yes, but we sometimes use the word 'reading' loosely.")

CONTROL QUALITY—*AND* HELPERS

Of course, clean up after yourself. Revise and proofread to catch any mistakes, including where spellcheck might have provided the wrong word. Ask someone, such as your English teacher, to check grammar, spelling, and punctuation—and only those elements.

Before you drop off the essay, guide your mentor in what to look for and what to overlook. Don't let them formalize the tone or change any opinions you've shared in the essay. The committee isn't judging you on some pre-conceived idea of the "right answer" to a question. If you need to, refer teachers to this section of the book and delicately explain that the college-admission process has changed since they went to school.

Also, limit the number of people who see your essay before you submit it. You don't want eighteen opinions on how to improve it. Ask a handful of people who know you best to read the essay and to reflect its main points and how you come across in it. If those points match your opening statement, you've done what you needed to do.

OH, %*@#!

I can't overstate the importance of reading, re-reading, and proofreading to make sure your essays reflect what you want to say. And be the final pair of eyes on it to prevent a true horror story like this:

One night at boarding school, the head school counselor ordered us to a meeting. Holding up a piece of paper and wearing the sternest-possible expression, he told us what this was about: He had just heard from Princeton University, and one of us had included an inappropriate essay. He proceeded to read it aloud.

There didn't seem to be anything wrong until he got to a certain point: *There* was the explicit language. The applicant seemed to be in shock. The counselor said he knew Matt hadn't written the offensive paragraph, so he asked what happened. That's when the student's also-horrified best friend explained that as a joke, he had added the paragraph when his friend left the room: "I thought he would've gone back and read it."

Parents are rarely the best mentors for essays, so you probably shouldn't share yours with them. They often try to control the story—"don't tell that one; tell *this* one"—add pressure, and impose a more mature style than is typical for a seventeen- or eighteen-year-old. They also often encourage a safer, less opinionated approach. But playing it safe won't get you into a top college.

I hope this goes without saying: Don't ask anyone to write the essay for you. Admissions committees have become adept at spotting essays written by someone who is older than eighteen. More important, this essay should reflect you, not anyone else's view of you. That's what recommendation letters are for.

With all of that said, try not to stress over writing the perfect essay. It doesn't have to change the world; it just needs to tell the committee about you. By following the tips in this chapter, your essays are likely to stand out, because most students aren't following these tips: They're starting too late and not giving their essays enough thought.

GIVE YOURSELF TIME

A shorter essay is more likely to be read, but not necessarily faster to write. In fact, it can take *longer* to write than a longer essay. A solid essay can sway the admissions committee, though, so dedicate plenty of time, thought, and effort to the project. Don't wait until the last minute. Essay writing is a process, not an event.

To ensure enough time to write an influential series of essays, start at the beginning of the summer before your senior year. Make and follow a timeline, if that seems useful to you. Brainstorm and bounce ideas off your friends and teachers—and maybe your parents if you're confident that they'll follow your lead and support your story. Write an outline. Then work through it a little at a time. Let it marinate, then come back to it. Don't revise until you've finished the rough draft.

THE TAKEAWAY

Particularly at some schools, a personal story that's consistent with the theme of your application will increase your chances of acceptance. Whether you start the application process with the essays or do them later, remember the key: Even if you think you're average, you have a story that only you can tell. Discover it by doing the exercises in this and the previous chapters.

THE FOLLOW-UP

The points you identified in your essays' pre-writing exercise will lead to talking points in your college interviews—the topic of the next chapter.

SIDEBAR QUESTIONS: HOW TO FIND THE COMPELLING FOCUS OF YOUR ESSAYS

A court case often rises or falls based on the personal testimony of the plaintiff or defendant. A strong performance on the stand can sway the most defiant jury or stubborn judge. The same is true for the personal essays in the college-admissions process. With so many students looking the same, essays represent your opportunity to take the stand and shine.

The following questions will help you identify a personal experience that might resonate with the admissions committee:

1. Review your opening statement. *What overall quality, skillset, or characteristic is your desired takeaway?*

2. Brainstorm any and all your stories, experiences, and/or activities. *Which best illustrate the desired takeaway from your opening statement?*

3. *Do any of the answers from Question #2 involve times of personal growth or struggle?*

4. Focus your attention on your answers to Question #3. *What was the precise moment you decided to push through the struggle?* Describe it in detail.

5. *How did this experience change you or your view of the world?*

CHAPTER 7

———

CROSS-EXAMINATION

STRENGTHENING YOUR CASE THROUGH ADMISSIONS INTERVIEWS

Although admissions interviews at most colleges are optional, if they're available, don't skip them. Take advantage of every opportunity to tell your story in front of the admissions committee, and note any questions they ask you. The experience will help you both improve your presentation and refine your list of schools.

From the school's perspective, just showing up for an interview demonstrates your interest and can set you apart from most of your peers. Your presence signals that you would be likely to accept an offer of admission, so *it boosts your chances of receiving one.*

You'll further distinguish yourself by being prepared, which few interviewees are. This story demonstrates the value of preparation: Jeremy was so worried about the admissions interview that he would have skipped it if he could. But his dream school, Georgetown University, is one of the few schools that require interviews of all applicants. To help him prepare, we met at a coffee shop to walk through a mock interview.

Before we began, I laid out this ground rule: "Act as if we're meeting for the first time." The student who, a moment before, had been relaxed, suddenly underwent a change in attitude. Now rigid and stammering, Jeremy gave a disjointed answer to my perennial first question, "Tell me about yourself."

Jeremy responded in the same way to my next question, one that's typical of college interviewers: "Why would you want to attend our college?" We weren't getting anywhere, so I stopped the interview and prompted him differently: "When we start over, pretend I'm your friend or a teacher you're comfortable around." Now Jeremy relaxed, and thoughts rolled off his tongue, highlighting key points from his resume. What had been random, rapid-fire phrases now came out in consistent flowing stories with a conversational tone.

The experience demonstrated the deficiencies I see with

a lot of students. By not knowing what to expect, they often fall off script and let their nerves take over. They miss the opportunity to learn about the school, they don't show their true selves, and they forget the key points they want to share.

Because you're reading this chapter, though, you'll know what to expect, and you'll have the tools to perform well.

WHAT TO EXPECT: INTERVIEW MECHANICS

For some schools that offer interviews, you don't have to ask for one The process tends to look like this: After you submit your application, and the school makes sure it's complete, you'll receive an email pairing you with an alum in your geographic area. In an area without alums, online communication services such as Skype or WebEx, or just the phone, may replace an in-person interview.

Some interviews take place on campus, and some schools foot the bill for these visits. Those schools fly in students who are "first gen"—a family's first generation to attend college. In addition to campus tours, the weekend visits typically include interview opportunities.

You may find other opportunities for interviews: When admissions-office representatives visit high schools in the fall, some offer interviews if you schedule them in advance. Keep in touch with your school counselor to learn which schools will be visiting and when you can expect those visits. These interviews are the best possible scenario because the interviewer is likely to be the one who'll later review your application file. Consider this your chance to put a face to your application and gain a champion for your cause.

Every school assigns an admissions representative to a particular region of the country. This rep will present at a college fair in every major metro area within that region. In the past, they've focused on private high schools, considered the "feeder" schools for elite universities. This selectivity is one more way in which universities have created an uneven playing field. More and more, though, universities have recognized the need to reach out to larger public schools.

AN OPPORTUNITY, NOT A CONFRONTATION

Your experience will vary depending on whether the interview is evaluative—and mandatory—or informative. You may be relieved to learn that at most schools, interviews are in the second category. These interviews exist only to inform students about the college and answer their questions.

In fact, very few schools give evaluative interviews. Of the top fifty nonmilitary schools in the U.S., only Georgetown and Yale require them. Those few will tell you about the interview well beforehand, so you'll have time to prepare accordingly. Another detail that should prevent you from exaggerating the weight and burden of even an evaluative interview is this: The interview represents only a small percentage of the university's admission criteria.

How small a percentage? The schools don't say exactly, but Georgetown's website does state this: "While the interview report is used as part of the admissions committee's consideration process, it rarely 'makes or breaks' an application, and, much more often than not, it works in the applicant's favor."[19] Of course that means you have nothing to fear from the interview. It might help your chances; it will rarely hurt them.

You might also take comfort in remembering that most universities see the primary purpose of every admissions interview as recruitment. They want to show applicants the human face of the university and to form a connection. The universities see this process as especially important for students who live too far away for a campus visit.

---

19   https://uadmissions.georgetown.edu/first-year/alumni-interview

PACK A POSITIVE ATTITUDE AND TONE

Go into both informative and evaluative interviews with a sense of curiosity and openness about the school. Consider them an opportunity to find out whether you and the school are a match. Also take advantage of the opportunity to find a mentor who went to the school you might attend.

The alum who interviews you might be a recent graduate, although that's not always the case. What you *can* expect is someone who is passionate about the university and is likely to promote it. Anticipate a positive, warm, and friendly tone, and respond in the same way.

Position yourself as the authority on yourself: No one knows more about you than you do. Use the interview to spotlight your strengths and successes throughout your high-school career. You've developed a clear and consistent opening statement. Before you walk into each interview, review it, your application file, and the key points you want to make.

TWELVE MORE INTERVIEWING TIPS

Planning and practice are the keys to finding your stride in every interview. In addition to improving your admissions interviews, you'll get better at interviews in general. That's a benefit that will pay off for all the interviews—with potential employers and maybe the news media—that you can expect throughout your life.

Before the interview—

1. RESEARCH THE COLLEGE

Although the purpose of the interview is to find out about the college, find out all you can before you step into the appointment. Learning about the school before you meet the interviewer will help you talk intelligently about why you're a fit and how you can contribute—what your goal is—particularly in an evaluative interview.

2. RESEARCH THE INTERVIEWER

If you learn the name of the interviewer in advance, find out when they graduated and what they're doing now. (You won't always learn the name in advance; if you don't, double your focus on the school itself.)

Also look for commonalities between you and the interviewer, which you can use as talking points to connect on a personal level. For example, if a web article by the interviewer demonstrates a love of baseball, a passion you authentically share, you can mention it as a jumping-off point.

Although your goal is to build rapport, recognize that you won't necessarily achieve it with every interviewer, and that isn't your fault. If you don't connect, continue to try. If that doesn't work, focus on presenting your story, learning what you can, and reminding yourself that the interview should not, in the words of Georgetown University, make or break your application. So, keep moving forward. In my grandmother's words, there's a reason a windshield is bigger than the rear-view mirror.

3. RESEARCH *YOURSELF*

Review your application and opening statement. For an evaluative interview, in particular, reduce your message to the "rule of three." Identify three main talking points that reflect your opening statement and spotlight your uniqueness. Three is the magic number, because studies of short-term memory have shown that, especially in stressful situations, a person can recall only that many things.

Researching yourself also means checking your social-media profile. One student I mock-interviewed did a brilliant job: She was relaxed and made me feel relaxed. She seemed like a strong prospect for her dream university. That was until I Googled her; the first photo showed this underage student holding a beer.

Remember that, in a way, you're always being interviewed through your always-accessible profiles and activities. Even if you're cautious about what you post about yourself, someone you know may not be. Do what you can to remove any posts that an admissions committee could view in a bad light.

In general, remain aware of the watchful eye of the Internet and the brand you're putting forward. Act as you want the world—which includes admissions officers, grandparents, and potential employers—to perceive you. When in doubt, leave it out and get a second trusted opinion. Also, continue to monitor your public presence throughout your life.

4. THINK THROUGH ANSWERS TO LIKELY QUESTIONS

"Think through" doesn't mean memorizing and reciting answers, which sounds unnatural. As you consider answers, identify talking points that reflect your application and yourself as an exceptional student. Interviews almost always include a variation of "Why are you interested in this college?" and "Tell me about yourself."

Your interviews might also include these typical questions:

- *What were your favorite courses in high school, and why did you like them?*

- *What did you enjoy most about high school?*
- *What challenges have you faced in life?*
- *How would you describe yourself to a stranger?*
- *How do you spend your free time?*
- *How do you spend your summers?*
- *Can you name a book you've read for fun in the past year?*
- *What can you tell me about yourself that's not in your application?*

If you feel as though you've poured your whole life into your application, that final question might trip you up, but it doesn't have to. Consider it an invitation to expand on an area you might have mentioned only briefly in your word-limited essay.

Also expect to field questions that aren't on this list, so take a look at #10 below for help with going into the interview in a relaxed state of mind.

5. PREPARE THOUGHTFUL QUESTIONS FOR YOUR INTERVIEWERS

Plan to ask about the alum's university career, college-choice criteria, and other questions that show your interest in the interviewer and, by association, the school.

6. PLAN LOGISTICS

Make sure you're clear on the exact interview time, location, transportation, and directions. Leave plenty of time for possible transit delays, and make sure you have gas in the car and parking instructions and money, or transit fare. If you can, make a trial run to the interview site.

Also, plan to be well-rested, well-fed, and well-hydrated but not wired on caffeine, so you're at your best throughout your interview.

7. DRESS NEATLY AND APPROPRIATELY

Present an appearance that's appropriate to the setting. In most cases, that translates to "church clothes" (as we used to say where I grew up): a solid long-sleeved blouse or shirt and slacks, a suit, or a business-like dress. *Don't* wear a t-shirt, jeans, or flip-flops.

8. ARRIVE A HALF-HOUR EARLY

Give yourself just enough time to make sure you're at the right place and can take a breath before the meeting. Consider that "*on* time is late," as my grandmother also used to say. Also avoid arriving too early at someone's office, or you might interfere with your interviewer's schedule. So, get to the area thirty minutes ahead, find a place to sit, review your notes, calm yourself, and show up for the interview five minutes early.

During the interview—

9. WATCH YOUR NONVERBAL LANGUAGE

When you meet the interviewer, shake hands and smile. Maintain eye contact throughout the interview, and keep your hands and legs relatively still.

10. RELAX

The more you practice, the more you're likely to relax. Some elite private schools offer interview coaching. If that's not available to you, take advantage of these other practice options in this order:

1. Start right now on one of the best ways to prepare for an interview: Practice speaking to people outside of your peer group and your school setting. I've found that students who are comfortable interacting with people of all ages and walks of life tend to relax and get more benefit out of interviews.
2. Then practice the admissions interview with supportive friends, parents, and teachers. Have them ask you typical admissions questions. Go through

several rounds until you start to get comfortable with the process.

3. Begin your actual interviews with schools that are lower on your list. In addition to working up to interviews for your dream school, these "practice" interviews might even improve a school's rank on your list.

11. CONVERSE

Your goal should be a give-and-take discussion: Ask questions as you go along, and avoid one-word answers that put the burden on the interviewer to keep the conversation going. Insert your three main points at natural places in the dialogue, and look for ways to build rapport with the interviewer.

Even though you're limiting your points to three memorable ones, bring along notes. Include your own copy of the activities sheet we discussed in Chapter 5, a copy of your transcript if it's exceptional, and anything else you think will help you in the moment.

Bring a note pad, and as the interviewer gives you helpful information, ask for permission to take notes, then, if permission is given, do so. The question tells the person that what they're saying is so valuable that you want to capture it in writing. Take notes with paper and pen, not a phone, laptop, or tablet, which will look to some interviewers as though you're not paying attention.

After the interview—

12. FOLLOW THROUGH AND FOLLOW UP

At the end of the interview, shake hands and thank the person for their time. Within twenty-four hours, send a thank-you letter, preferably on paper by mail. Use the letter to jog the interviewer's memory about your meeting and about you; they may have interviewed several people in the past week. Your notes will help with this, too. For example, if you chatted about baseball, you might say something like, "It was great to talk about the Phillies' baseball season with you." You could even include a newspaper or magazine article that's relevant to your conversation.

THE TAKEAWAY

That conversation—your interview—is your way to show you're truly interested in a college and to learn more about it. You can derive benefits that many of your peers won't. Most students don't choose to attend interviews, and, of the ones who do, most let nerves get in their way.

Take the opportunity and prepare to make the most of the experience.

THE FOLLOW-UP

At this point in the book, you've built your case: You've identified your strengths, gathered a list of schools that fit you, pulled together your witness list, and learned how to ace admissions interviews. You're ready to actually apply. The information you need now is coming up in the next chapter.

SIDEBAR QUESTIONS: HOW TO EXPLOIT YOUR INTERVIEW OPPORTUNITIES

If an attorney's client testifies during a trial, the opposing attorneys will have the chance during cross-examination to scrutinize the client's case and credibility. The college admissions interview—although not adversarial—provides a similar opportunity to better understand a student's case for admissions.

Consider the following questions:

1. *Do any colleges on your list offer admissions interviews?* If so, seize these opportunities and make the most of them.

2. *Are the interviews evaluative or informative?* Make sure you adequately prepare, in particular, for all evaluative interviews.

3. *Who at each college typically interviews the applicant—for example, is it an alum, a student, or an admissions representative?* If possible, try to learn the name of your interviewer, so you can fully research them before the interview.

4. Review your opening statement. *What overall quality, skillset, or characteristic is your desired takeaway? What three talking points best illustrate it?* Again, your interview answers should reinforce your case for admissions.

5. *What remaining questions do you have about the specific college?* At some point, the interviewer will ask for your questions. Make sure that these questions are ones that aren't easily answered by the college's website.

CHAPTER 8

JURY DELIBERATION AND FINAL VERDICT

SUBMITTING YOUR APPLICATION AND ACCEPTING THE RIGHT OFFER OF ADMISSION

To move from the schools that initially interested you to the ones to which you'll ultimately apply, begin by revisiting and possibly updating your priorities. With the help of this chapter, you'll overlay those priorities with the types of applications that are available at the universities that interest you. Finally, you'll determine the best fit for your interests, financial situation, and academic record.

Even though your parents should weigh in on financial considerations and can offer guidance and feedback, it bears repeating that you should be the one deciding where to apply and which offer to accept. You're the one who will live on that campus for the next four years. You're the one who will live the life that your college career will help shape.

To help you in this key decision, review and update the notes, the list, and the matrix you made in Chapter 2 of what matters most to you in your choice of college. See whether your interests have changed in the year since you made these notes. For many students, senior year is a time of growth and change—as a student and as a person—and it probably is for you, too.

So, re-examine the schools on your list through an updated lens. Do they offer the major and courses that interest you *now*? Are you still comfortable with their environments? Have your extracurricular interests changed, and can you pursue them at these schools?

If you're still unsure where to apply, you may need to do more research to compare and contrast your finalists. Return to the suggestions in Chapter 2.

Recognize that the process of deciding where to apply takes time, so build in plenty of it. In most cases, that means you should plan on narrowing your final list *early* in your senior year. Depending on your situation, you might also be wise to *apply* early. Doing so will set you apart and boost your chances of finding a champion in the admissions committee, for three reasons:

1. Applying early puts your file in a different, more attractive application pool than the hordes that will show up later.
2. Your file is more likely to be seen by an admissions officer who is *rested*—who has not read hundreds of applications in one month.
3. "Early decision," one type of early-admissions application, shows your interest in the university, as you'll see in the following section.

THREE TYPES—AND TIMES—OF APPLICATIONS

"Early" describes an application that arrives well before the crowd. But you may need to consider other pros and cons in deciding when to apply.

1. REGULAR ADMISSIONS

Most students wait to apply until the "regular admissions" deadline. At many schools, that's January 1st of the students' senior year. An application at this date brings response—acceptance, denial, or waitlist—in late March or early April and requires a decision by May 1st.

Of course, even regular-admissions applications can come too early: Sarah is one student who didn't discover her career passion—marine biology—until the *spring* of her senior year of high school, *after* she had applied to colleges. Her list included only two colleges with any course offerings in the topic. Both colleges had been low on her list before her exposure to marine biology. She accepted one of them.

The lesson here is to stay flexible in your choice of schools and experiment with topics as much and as early as you can. (Sarah's newfound interest came about randomly, however. She took that marine-biology class at her local community college only because it was all that fit in her spring schedule.)

2. ROLLING ADMISSIONS

Possibly later still are "rolling admissions" applications that public universities may offer. In this case, the student can apply at almost any time and receive a response after four to eight weeks. Schools that accept this type of application often do so until they fill their class. In some cases, that's just before the term begins in the fall. If a public university is on your safety-school list, a rolling admission can give you the confidence boost of your first acceptance letter.

3. EARLY ACCEPTANCE

If you have a first-choice school whose academic threshold you meet, I recommend one of the "early acceptance" options, the third type of application. This can bring a response as soon as December 15th. To apply this way, though, you'll need to identify that first choice early in your senior year, because the application deadline for early acceptance is November 1st or 15th. Types of early acceptance include "early decision" and "early action."

With **early decision**, you apply to one college with the understanding that if it accepts you, you must attend: It's a binding agreement. That fact proves interest in the university, so it raises your chances of acceptance—by as much as two to three times over the regular-admissions process. (The one escape hatch of early-decision's binding agreement is a financial-aid offer that is woefully inadequate. However, this is a high hurdle that is rarely cleared.)

With **early *action***, you don't show as much love for the school as you do with early decision, but it does allow freedom and time: You're not bound to attend, and you can take until May 1st—the same deadline as for regular admissions—to decide whether you will.

FOLLOW THE MONEY

If you need financial aid and don't meet the academic thresholds of colleges with the best no-loan financial-aid offers, steer clear of early decision. Early decision also isn't the best option even if you do meet these thresholds, because it deprives you of the ability to receive and choose among multiple financial-aid offers.

Early decision also lowers bargaining power. Let's say you receive a better financial-aid offer from your second-choice school. If the school is similarly ranked and viewed as a competitor to your first choice, your first choice might consider matching the other offer. If you can, ask your parent to contact the financial-aid office. In fact, financial aid is one of the few admissions areas in which I recommend that your family get involved. Your parent may be in a better position to discuss financial need than you are.

UPON ACCEPTANCE, YOU'RE IN CHARGE: HOW TO CHOOSE

Before and during your application process, you were trying to make your case to the schools. As soon as they decide to accept your application, the pendulum of power swings back to you.

By following the lessons in this book, you should have the

great "problem" of more than one acceptance letter to choose from. To compete for your acceptance of their offers, schools are likely to double their efforts to persuade you to attend. As I mentioned in an earlier chapter, their ranking in terms of *yield rate* depends on having their offers accepted. Don't allow yourself to be swayed at the last moment by their marketing or by the appeal of wearing a particular college's sweatshirt for the prestige it might convey.

Take your time to accept an offer; you have nothing to gain by rushing. Remember, your reply—to regular-admission or early-action acceptance—isn't due until May 1st. As when you compiled your initial school list and later when you narrowed it to applications, think through the pros and cons of each school that accepted you and remember why you applied in the first place.

If you didn't tour the schools before, if you possibly can, try to visit the finalists among the schools that have accepted you. Just as you probably wouldn't buy a house without a walk-through and inspection, or a car without a test drive, avoid buying into a university until you've set foot on campus. The investment in your education could be worth hundreds of thousands of dollars, so it merits an intensive level of scrutiny.

Even if you toured early in your process, the lens through

which you view the school *after* you're accepted may become sharper. One more opportunity to tour a campus and gather decision-supporting material may come in April, when a lot of schools offer orientations or open houses for admitted students. Attending such orientations has sold some students and—despite the school's goal of persuasion—turned off others.

This decision can be really tough. Two days before the decision deadline, I spent three hours on the phone with Karen, who was struggling to pick between two schools—her choice versus her parents'. She wanted to accept the small private liberal-arts school that fit her better: She preferred the size of the school and the town. The school offered more programs that interested her, as well as research opportunities and interaction with faculty. It *also* offered her a better financial-aid package than her parents' favorite.

Karen's parents, on the other hand, had always envisioned her going to a particular university—it was even the logo on the onesie she wore soon after she was born. It was where she was "supposed" to go, but Karen didn't see herself at a school where the student population is 30,000 and an introductory class might hold 700 students. But she had not had that conversation with her parents.

Ultimately, every parent wants what's best for their child,

and what's best is what makes them happy, so I encouraged Karen to take a stand. I advised her that if she had completed all her research, and if this small college felt like where she belonged, she needed to make the case to her parents. She did, they agreed, and she'll head to the school of her choice in September.

If you're also struggling to choose among schools, I hope that, after weighing all the factors, you step into your decision and embrace it. If you still can't make up your mind, consider this: Where you go to college does not dictate whom you'll ultimately become. You can get a great education anywhere, and ultimately, there's no wrong choice.

I have worked on Supreme Court cases with brilliant people who went to colleges you've never heard of. In fact, I've worked with talented people from various backgrounds through every step of my career. You get to decide who you are based on your work ethic. Although some colleges may provide you with an advantage early in your career, your perseverance and character will drive you further than the university name on your diploma.

What's more, if, after making a choice and giving the school a fair trial, you're unhappy, see whether you can switch majors or find some activity that will improve your well-being there. If not, you might find you need to transfer. Life is too short to spend four unhappy years in college.

A transfer should be the last resort, though. You're better off picking an acceptable college right out of high school for a couple of reasons: There's some evidence that transfer students don't receive financial-aid packages that are as generous as new students do. Also, if your unhappiness has led to poor grades, you may have trouble selling yourself to a comparable college.

THE TAKEAWAY

When it comes time to apply to colleges, keep your priorities straight. Focus on what's important to *you*—not to your parents, teachers, or peers. Your priorities should drive your decision on where to apply and which offer to accept. Make sure they're clear in your mind by reviewing the homework you did on yourself. Continue to return to your priorities to keep your decision process simple and honest—unlike those of students who develop convoluted formulas including weighted factors.

To help you focus on your priorities, make sure you avoid getting lost in the details you might learn from the schools themselves, such as the number of books in the library, the dimension of dorm rooms, or the percentage of donating alumni. Not every factor deserves equal weight. One student based his decision on food: "At this campus, it's all you can eat twenty-four hours a day; someone will make me an omelet at 3 a.m.!" I responded, "Denny's offers that, too. Should that really drive your decision on where to go to college?" But it did, because that's what was important to him. No one should judge your priorities.

One of Karen's reasons for her private-school choice was that her friends were all going there. You're better off *not* choosing a school just because your boyfriend, girlfriend, or friends are going there. You'll make new friends in your new school, and, in the case of a boy- or girlfriend, you might break up over Christmas. Even if you don't break up, consider college an opportunity to broaden your circle of friends, and consider stronger factors, as Karen ultimately did.

Also, resist the temptation to procrastinate. If you can identify your top choice or choices early in the process, and if the schools offer early acceptance, take advantage of that option.

THE FOLLOW-UP

You've worked through the valuable process of identifying and building your strengths, unique story, key witnesses, academic evidence, and dream schools. You've applied where you belong. In fact, you've done everything you can to overcome the obstacles between you and your best college destination.

Let's revisit the courtroom analogy once more to imagine a jury that's more likely to side with a person of a particular socioeconomic background or race. It's unfair, but it's often the reality. In a real sense, college-admissions committees act like such juries. To be successful, you must use what you know about them to build a case they'll welcome. Tell a story that's consistent, from your evidence through witness testimony and cross-examination.

As this book has shown you, you must prove you are an exceptional student. Examine yourself and your chosen colleges to highlight how well you fit together. Evaluate the options you've received based on your identity, preferences, and needs.

You're fortunate that you've found the underground playbook that some people don't want you to have. With this book, you've also found a way past the gatekeepers onto a more level playing field. You now know the secrets of boosting your odds of getting into the college you want. If you do even *half* of what this book advises, you have a chance to succeed. I wish you *every* success. Go out and get what's yours.

Recognize that so many other students will follow the flock onto a path that leads to nowhere—a college that doesn't fit them. Have the courage to take your own stand and make this playbook work for you. When you do use its resources to defy the odds and get into the college of your dreams—the one that everyone said you couldn't *touch*—I hope you'll share your personal success stories with Jeb@CollegeAdmissions.com. Until then, check the website frequently for additional resources.

SIDEBAR QUESTIONS: HOW TO DECIDE WHERE TO APPLY

Timing is everything in the courtroom. The same is often true in the college-admissions process. Because many colleges give the edge to students who apply early, consider when and where to submit your application.

These questions will guide you:

1. Research the application options and deadlines for all the colleges on your list. *Do any of them offer an early-application option (early action or early decision)? Do any of them offer rolling admissions? What are the key deadlines?*

2. *Do any of these colleges offer only early decision (which means if you're accepted, you agree to go to that school)? If so, are any of these colleges your absolute top choice and offer only loan-free financial aid?* Don't apply for early decision unless both statements are true or money is not a concern. Otherwise, you could find yourself committed to a school that exceeds your budget.

3. *If you are deferred or wait-listed, what supplemental information can you send the college?* The admissions committee is still deliberating your case, so use the opportunity to update them on your recent success.

4. To make an educated decision about where to go to college, fully evaluate each college, beginning by reviewing your initial list of colleges. *Why did each college make the list in the first place? Have your interests or priorities changed over the months? Are you able to visit each college that accepted you?*

5. *What college feels right to **you**?* Your parents, friends, and teachers can advise you, but you're the one who will attend classes and spend the next four years at the college.

APPENDIX 1

HIGH-SCHOOL TIMELINE AND CHECKLIST FOR
APPLICATIONS ACTIVITIES: WHEN TO DO WHAT
IN YOUR *FRESHMAN* YEAR—

☐ Think about short- and long-term personal and academic goals. Discuss your goals with your school counselor, teachers, and possibly parents. Revisit your goals regularly and revise them based on your changing interests and priorities.

☐ Discuss your four-year course schedule with your school counselor. Identify courses that help you further your unique interests.

☐ Pursue extracurricular activities that help you explore your unique interests and talents.

☐ Proactively seek projects and initiatives that improve your school and your community.

- ☐ Meet with your teachers outside of class time, so you can better understand the material and your teachers can better appreciate your passion for their subject matter.
- ☐ Start to think about possible types of colleges that might interest you. For example, visit local colleges to get a feel for the different types of campuses: urban versus rural and large versus small, for example.
- ☐ Keep a journal of your activities and accomplishments. To identify unique interests and trends, and to help you build your case for college admissions, update your journal monthly throughout high school.

IN YOUR *SOPHOMORE* YEAR—

- ☐ In September, register for the October PSAT. Also consider taking the PLAN, if it's available.
- ☐ Keep your grades high and carry the most challenging course load you can. If you stumbled academically during your freshman year, start the upward trend this year.
- ☐ Deepen your interests and commitment to unique extracurricular activities. Drop any activities that distract your attention from your passions.
- ☐ Start to visit colleges that interest you. Keep a file on each school. (For a template, see Appendix 2.)
- ☐ Revisit and revise your personal and academic goal list.

- ☐ Meet with your school counselor to discuss your short- and long-term academic and personal interests. Ask about any potential programs and projects that would allow you to further explore what interests you.
- ☐ Find summer activities that let you sample your career interests.
- ☐ Dedicate sufficient time during the summer months to study for the ACT, PSAT, and SAT.
- ☐ Continue updating your journal of activities and accomplishments on a monthly basis. Find any evolving trends or developments in your unique interests and talents.

IN YOUR *JUNIOR* YEAR—

- ☐ Revisit and revise your list of personal and academic goals.
- ☐ Meet with your school counselor to discuss academic progress, current interests, and your list of potential colleges.
- ☐ Continue focusing on your coursework.
- ☐ Take on leadership roles in your extracurricular activities. Make and track tangible improvements you have made.
- ☐ Visit the websites of all the colleges you're considering. Request catalogs and financial aid information, and expand and update your file on each college.

- ☐ Identify potential private-scholarship opportunities, if you want them, and when the applications are due. (But again, if you need financial aid, don't waste your valuable time applying for private scholarships. They are rarely worth the effort, and the schools may reduce your financial aid by the amount of the private scholarship.)
- ☐ Attend local and virtual college fairs.
- ☐ Visit all colleges that interest you, if you can.
- ☐ Take the PSAT in the fall to potentially qualify for National Merit status.
- ☐ Take the SAT and ACT at least once during your junior year. Register at least six weeks before the date of the test. If you can't afford the test, ask for a fee waiver. Prepare for the test as if for a course. Be sure to schedule daily study time and regularly take practice tests.
- ☐ Attend online and in-person workshops about financial aid.
- ☐ Find a summer internship or some other opportunity to pursue your unique area of interest.
- ☐ Register for the SAT Subject Tests in the subjects that you are currently studying in school.
- ☐ Take the AP exam for every AP course you're taking.
- ☐ Obtain applications for scholarships.
- ☐ Update and review your journal of accomplishments and activities.

- ☐ Approach teachers about writing college recommendations.
- ☐ Retake the SAT or the ACT if you didn't score high enough to get into your target colleges.
- ☐ Continue updating your journal of activities and accomplishments. Find any evolving trends or developments in your unique interests and talents.
- ☐ Start working on your personal essays for college applications.

IN YOUR *SENIOR* YEAR—

- ☐ Revisit and revise your list of personal and academic goals.
- ☐ Meet with your school counselor to discuss your academic progress, current interests, and your list of potential colleges.
- ☐ Mark your calendar with when to register and take standardized tests, send college applications, and apply for financial aid. Review this calendar on a weekly basis.
- ☐ Retake the SAT or the ACT if you didn't score high enough to get into your target colleges.
- ☐ Download financial aid and college applications for each school on your list. You can download the common application after August 1st.
- ☐ Finish your college essays.

- ☐ Review your high-school transcript for any errors. Discuss any discrepancies or low grades with your school counselor.
- ☐ Attend college fairs and workshops on financial aid to learn of any recent developments.
- ☐ Visit any remaining schools on your target list.
- ☐ Schedule interviews if your target schools offer them.
- ☐ Request letters of recommendations from teachers, counselors, and coaches.
- ☐ Complete all college applications well before the deadlines.
- ☐ Apply early if all the criteria identified in Chapter 8 are met.
- ☐ Apply to the remaining schools on your target list.
- ☐ Verify that each college received a complete application, including letters of recommendation and ACT or SAT test scores.
- ☐ Compile all the documentation needed for your financial aid application.
- ☐ In January, send your financial-aid applications and mid-year grades to colleges.
- ☐ Revisit your top-choice colleges after you receive acceptance letters.
- ☐ Compare financial-aid offers.
- ☐ Discuss college offers with your school counselor.
- ☐ If you're wait-listed, contact the admissions representative with any developments in your academic

or extracurricular pursuits. Supply additional documentation, if needed.

☐ Wait to hear from all the colleges you applied to before you accept an offer of admission.

☐ By May 1st, accept the offer from your top choice and send in your enrollment deposit by FedEx or UPS. Verify housing application deadlines and refund procedures. Pay necessary deposits.

☐ Notify the other colleges of your decision.

☐ Update your counselor and teachers on your decision. Send thank-you letters to everyone who helped you during the process.

☐ Keep your grades up through graduation. Verify that a final copy of your transcript is sent to your college.

☐ Celebrate!

APPENDIX 2

COLLEGE CHARACTERISTICS

Fill out a copy of this form for every school you consider, so you can easily recall and compare schools throughout your college search.

NAME OF SCHOOL:

Location:

College Website:

Admissions Office Contact Information:

PROFILE OF RECENTLY ADMITTED STUDENTS

Number of applications received?

% of all applicants admitted?

Number of early
applications received?

Acceptance rate of early
applicant pool?

% of admitted class filled through
early-application process?

GPA: % of admitted students in
top 10% of their high school class?

GPA: % of admitted students in
top 20% of their high school class?

GPA: % of admitted students in
top 50% of their high school class?

SAT: mid-50% math score?

SAT: mid-50% reading
& writing score?

ACT: mid-50% composite score?

STANDARDIZED-TEST SPECIFICATIONS
(REQUIRED, RECOMMENDED, OPTIONAL)

SAT?

ACT?

SAT essay?

ACT essays?

SAT subject tests?

APPLICATION PROCESS

Application deadlines?

Type of early application?
(early action, binding early
decision, rolling admissions)

Teacher recommendations
required?

Interviews available? If so,
evaluative or informative?

Customized or common
application?

Common application
supplemental essays?

FINANCIAL AID

Guarantees to meet full demonstrated need?

Offers merit aid?

Offers need-blind admissions?

Offers only need-based aid?

Offers no-loan financial aid?

Do private scholarships affect the amount of financial-aid offers?

FAFSA deadline?

CSS profile deadline?

Other relevant deadlines? (e.g., school-supplied scholarships that might require separate applications)

CAMPUS CONSIDERATIONS

Setting? (urban, suburban, or rural?)

School category? (research university, liberal-arts college, or other?)

Enrollment?

Requires on-campus housing for freshmen?

Guarantees on-campus housing for all four years?

% of students living on campus?

% of students living off-campus but within two miles of the campus?

% of students living more than two miles from campus?

Student demographics? (e.g., male-to-female ratio, racial diversity, political diversity)

Social life? (e.g., % of students in fraternities or sororities or in various on-campus activities)

Other considerations? (e.g., curriculum, available extracurricular activities, academic rigor, special programs of interest)

OVERALL IMPRESSION

Overall impression?

APPENDIX 3

SAMPLE ACTIVITIES SHEET

Enrico Mancino
123 Briarwood Circle
Philadelphia, PA 19107
(215) 123-4567
JoeSmith@email.com

OPENING STATEMENT

Something unique about my life is that I help my mother raise my three younger siblings while my father serves a life sentence in prison. My academic strengths include a 33 ACT composite score, a 3.6 weighted overall GPA, and a perfect 4.0 in math and science classes. Outside of the classroom, I have made my mark in my community by starting an outreach program for children of incarcerated parents, leading my classmates as Junior and Senior Class President, and founding a Bocce Ball Team, all while working 16 hours/week at a pediatric psychiatrist's office. Others would describe me as a caring, passionate, hard-working person, who pushes others to reach their full potential. In the future, I plan to become a pediatric psychiatrist, with a special focus on helping children overcome the mental angst of parental incarceration.

ACADEMIC METRICS

Weighted Overall GPA (through junior year): 3.6

Unweighted Overall GPA (through junior year): 3.3

SAT Math Score: 720

SAT Evidence-Based Reading & Writing Score: 680

ACT Composite Score: 33

AP Exams: Chemistry (4), Biology (5), Calculus AB (5), English Language & Composition (3)

IMPACT

The following list spotlights some of the measurable results I have helped achieve outside the classroom. This list does not include all my accomplishments—only those that have been most meaningful to me, my family, and my community.

SCHOOL ACTIVITIES

Class President 11, 12 (~3 hours/week during school year)
Elected by Junior class after only three weeks at new school. Obtained funding for twelve new clubs that serve the surrounding community. Re-elected senior year based on inclusive platform of tearing down societal walls separating students. Convinced school administration to use electronic card system to conceal who is on free lunch program. Local news station covered progress.

Founder/Coach of Bocce Ball Team 11, 12 (~5 hours/week during school year)
Introduced student body to sport from my native Italy. Received official school recognition as varsity sport after club team won regional tournament. Organized youth camp to introduce sport to community.

COMMUNITY SERVICE

Founder of Outreach for Children of Incarcerated Parents (OCIP) 11, 12 (~3 hours/week year-round)
Received funding after presenting idea to city council. Worked closely with local court system to promote program services. Meet weekly with other children of incarcerated parents. Discussed success of program on *Good Morning America*.

Boys & Girls Club of America Math & Sciences Tutor 9, 10, 11, 12 (~2 hours/ week during school year)

Share passion for math and sciences with elementary-school children. Teach monthly "Not Taught in School" science class to third-grade students. Recognized as "Tutor of the Year" during my Junior year.

WORK/SUMMER EXPERIENCE

Administrative Assistant, Pediatric Psychiatric Associates 11, 12 (16 hours/ week year-round)

Work eight hours/day on Saturday and Sunday. Interact with pediatric psychiatrist who specializes in PTSD in children of incarcerated parents. Re-organized record-keeping system to streamline patient management.

Aspirations

My current long-term career plans are to launch a pediatric psychiatric facility where children of incarcerated parents can receive proper care. In the short term, I hope to attend a university with a strong psychology department that encourages student involvement in cutting-edge research. It would be a major plus if the university had a competitive bocce ball team.

ABOUT THE AUTHOR

JEB WHITE is the founder of CollegeAdmissions.com. Despite growing up in a working-class family, he earned an undergraduate degree from an Ivy League institution and a law degree from a top law school—along with the blessing of financial stability.

Jeb is a widely sought-after speaker, having appeared at universities, on CNBC and NPR stations, and in other news outlets, including the *New York Times*, the *Wall Street Journal*, and *Bloomberg News*. His appearances, published works, videos, and college-admissions programs motivate thousands around the world.

10358328R00108

Made in the USA
Monee, IL
28 August 2019